DORICULA

THE PRINCE OF

C000078505

Or, "Fan Cheryl and Clint Went First Place"

By Mike Jamieson

Based on the (so-called) comedy stage play "Doricula" by Mike Jamieson; itself loosely based on the novel "Dr. Acula" by Bam Stoker (1897).

Dedicated to Charles Barron (1936-2012) and to my mum, Elizabeth (Betty) Jamieson (1929 – 2011).

With explanatory footnotes; and a glossary of 'Aiberdeen' words and terms.

Published in the United States by **Beowulf Publishing**, Houston, Texas.

Library of Congress Cataloging-in-Publication data are available upon request.

ISBN: 978-0692439517

Cover Art by Mike Jamieson. The silhouettes are, from the left, the Salvation Army Citadel, The Town House and King's College.

By the same author:
Dr. Fa and the Dorics (Beowulf Publishing, Houston, Texas 2016)

Michael J Jamieson, Houston, Texas, 2016 www.mikejjamieson.com
Visit 'Doricula' on facebook.

Synopsis

The first Gothic novel to be set in Aberdeen *and* Cluj, Doricula is a story of unrequited love, lust, greed, terror and rowies. Former Northeast lovers Cheryl and Clint, long-separated by the unspeakable horrors of the Second World War (and by the speakable horror of Cheryl's marriage to their mutual chum, Wallfield), are reunited after seventy-four years, while waiting in line at the bakery counter at Morrison's. Their tragic tale chronicles yet another horror: a centuries-old quest by Count Vlad Doricula ("The Prince of Doricness") to claim dominion over Aberdeen, and reclaim its Common Good Fund. Along the way the threesome go first fitting in Transylvania, almost go ice-skating at Garthdee, right some of the countless wrongs inflicted on the City by generations of clueless Planning Committees, and – with the help of a failed proctologist – try to avert a fiendish Nazi plot, masterminded by a local Vampire hunter.

About the Author

Mike Jamieson was born in Aberdeen at a very young age. Unfortunately, his mum couldn't be present at the birth, having wraxed her back taking in a bucket of coal. According to his dad, Jim, "That wid nivver a' happened wi' Shilbottle". He was educated at Aberdeen Grammar School and received his Medical degree from Aberdeen University in 1980. As a child he was fascinated by the Hammer horror films, but his mum wouldn't let him bide up and watch them.

Mike's parents experienced at first hand the German Luftwaffe raids on Aberdeen, including the bombing of Hall Russell shipyard and properties in Urquhart Road, Roslin Street and Jasmine Terrace (where his dad lived – as did Mike, for his first six weeks) on July 12, 1940.

Mike has been involved in Doric (or more accurately, 'Aiberdeen') comedy in some fashion since appearing in a tinfoil wig in the 1976 Aberdeen Student Show, 'A Just in Time'. Mike is author of 'Doctor Fa and the Dorics'. He maintains the facebook groups 'Doric', 'Aberdeen Student Show Centennial', and 'Aiberdeen 2017 UK City a' Culcher'. He has three sons, all graduates of Robert Gordon's College, lives in Houston, Texas, and stays up as late as he wants.

Acknowledgments

To my dad, James Jamieson - much love and many thanks for the incredible first hand reminiscences about the events of July 12, 1940, and insights into the Aiberdeen Illuminati.

Thanks to Eric Crockart, who suggested the title (instead of the original 'Coont Dracula'). And to my long-time collaborator, Gary Simpson, who coauthored the original 'Exorcist' sketch, inspiration for the confession scene in Chapter 11.

Many thanks also to my middle son, Daniel Jamieson, for invaluable editorial comments.

I would also like to thank Alex Jones, whose original gothic photographs of Aberdeen's rooftops by moonlight helped inspire the cover art.

Finally I would like to thank Haider Hassan (aka Haider Gottfried), founder of Beowulf Publishing, who originally persuaded me to convert the play 'Dr Fa and the Thing from Outer Speyside' into our first e-book, 'Dr Fa and the Dorics'. This is our second attempt to work out the kinks.

A Word or Two Aboot the Language

'Doric' (or 'The Doric') nowadays refers to the rich indigenous dialect of Northeast Scotland, having previously referred to the dialects of the Scottish Lowlands and Northumbria. Doric may have originated as a joking parallel reference (by some bright spark at Oxbridge) to the dialect of the Dorian Greeks of Sparta, who were regarded by the Athenian Greeks as minkers (see Glossary).

Other than introductions and footnotes, 'Doricula' is largely written in 'Aberdeen', or 'Aiberdeen', the urban dialect of the City of Aberdeen. Aiberdeen and Doric are related but distinct. Aiberdeen is a lazier dialect, frequently shortening and truncating words. There is no standard spelling of Aiberdeen (nor, for that matter, Doric); accordingly phonetic spellings differ. For example the English 'all' is pronounced as the single harder vowel 'a', which may be spelled aa, aah, ah, or a'. There are many online references and glossaries for both dialects, but for those unfamiliar with either, a few features of Aiberdeen that appear in this book include:

- The initial 'wh' is shortened to 'f' in words such as 'fa' (who), 'far' (where) and 'fan' (when).
- Consonants - particularly g, l, n and t - are dropped within and at the end of words. 'Deeing' (doing) becomes deein'. 'Canna' (can't) becomes ca'. Fall becomes fa'. 'Fittie' (Footdee) is glottalized to 'fi'y'.
- 'Ou' becomes 'oo', as in 'doot' (doubt), and 'oot an' aboot'.
- The diminutive 'ie' is common – 'bussie' (bus fare), 'loonie' ('loon' (boy)), 'quinie' ('quine' (girl)).

A Glossary of words and phrases appearing in this book, along with some other common words, is included at the end.

Characters (in order of appearance)

Barnes Noble	Cheryl's dad, married to her mum, Bunty.
Reverend Deverend Vale	Minister of St Machar's Cathedral.
Offstage Voice	During the Minister's introduction
Announcer	PA in Morrison's supermarket.
Cheryl Noble	Clint's girlfriend.
Clint Eastneuk	Cheryl's boyfriend.
Wallfield	Clint's friend and colleague.
Donnie J Macleodmouth	Disastermind Quizmaster.
Coont Doricula	Vlad, the Vampire.
Arthur Bean	Transylvanian coach and taxi driver.
Operator	Cluj Telecom
Abraham Van Hazelheid	Lord Provost and Vampire Hunter.
Brother Duthie	Member of the Woolmanhillati.
Brother Benzie	Another member of the Woolmanhillati.
Brother Craigmyle	Another member of the Woolmanhillati.
Brother Giulianotti	Another member of the Woolmanhillati.
Brother Esslemont	Another member of the Woolmanhillati.
Brother Hall	Another member of the Woolmanhillati.
Brother Wood	Another member of the Woolmanhillati.
Dr. John Kingseat	Retired proctologist and Vampire Expert.

Chronology

Background

The legend of the Vampire is ingrained in the northeast Scottish psyche. Whose mother hasn't crept into the kids' bedroom at 2 am, after a win at the Cheval, to terrify them with a Dracula impression?

At the slight risk of political incorrectness, Aberdonians have never liked continentals. Never mind your 'Twin Cities'. Forget your Clermont-Ferrands, Gomels and Stavangers. Keep your Regensburg Week. And as for your Bulawayos – far the hell is that onywye? Aberdeen especially dislikes foreigners with better fitba teams (i.e. them all).

Aberdonian parents in the Sixties were early adopters of the stylish EKCO T345 Black & White television. Thirteen settings on the dial (two channels available), valves replaced only every three weeks by the mannie with the big suitcase from Telemech (not to be confused with the Betterwear mannie with the little wee floor polish samples).

And so a generation of Aberdonians grew up on Hammer Film Productions' classic and highly accurate biopics: 'Dracula'. 'The Curse of Frankenstein', 'The Mummy', 'The Curse of the Werewolf', 'The Gorgon' and 'One Million Years BC'. Accordingly, adult Aberdonians harbour deep distrust of Pterodactyls, Transylvanians, loons with outdated leather jackets hanging around the Thainstone Mart, gypsies (sorry, 'travellers') and Vampires.

Vampirism has never caught on in Aberdeen. Never mind the claustrophobia: cremation is half the price. Cremation took forever to catch on too - Aberdonians couldn't stand to burn a perfectly good box. Until it became far too expensive, Aberdonians preferred interment, preferably at Trinity Cemetery (for the view). Nowadays, plots (burial, vegetable or both) are also in short supply. However, if the 'vision' of certain un-named local billionaires is realized, and central Aberdeen is 'revitalized' (God forbid), the St. Nicholas Graveyard will be dug up for parking, freeing up space on the Union Street side for a few multi-storey burial plots, as well as desperately-needed mobile phone shops.

Anyway, back to our tale, which is set in and around Aberdeen, Dunkirk and Cluj, Transylvania, between 1938 and the present day. In a few minutes, our Master of Ceremonies, the minister, will take us through the chronology. But, first, imagine you have the best seat in the Orchestra Stalls at His Majesty's Theatre. Which, to be honest, is an oxymoron unless you're five foot six or shorter. The script, stage directions, musical and sound effect cues are in your hand. The lights dim, the audience hushes, the front tabs part slightly, a solitary lime lights, revealing a uniformed man, flat on his back, writing a letter to his wife …

Prologue – May 26, 1940

A foxhole in the beach at Dunkirk, France.

Barnes Noble, wearing the uniform of a sapper, is writing a letter with a tiny pencil on a scrap of paper.

[Sound effect: distant explosions]
[Sound effect: waves breaking on sand]

Barnes: (slowly – he is writing as he speaks to himself)

World War … eh, Two.
British Expeditionary Force, Dunkirk Beach and Leisure Centre. Frunce.
The twinty sixth a' May, nineteen hunner and forty.
Three fifty-nine pm. Near aboot.

Dear Bunty:

I hope this letter finds you weel, and nae deid.

Please gie oor little bairn, Cheryl, a big bosie. Tell her I hinna forgotten her birthday. Although I canna mind if it's her 63rd or 64th.

I hinna picked oot a present yet, but I'm ga'n to Calais the mor'n. I'll probably bide the night. There's rare hotel there – the Calais Thistle.

There's nae decent clies shops in Dunkirk. Nithing like Aiberdeen. I've looked a'wye for a Millet's. Or an Issac Benzies. There's nae even a Rae's. Far they get their Wranglers fae, or their school uniforms, I've nae idea. Unfortunately there's nae a Rubber Shop - so I'll just hae to keep scoring oot.

This may be my last message for a whiley, as I've run oot a' Dazzle bottles ti pit them in.

Div you mind my pal Cyril? That works at the Castlegate lavvies? Selling French letters? The ither kind. The een that did the splits on a palin' fan he wis a loon? It turns oot he's an expert on groins. Baith kinds. Well, he telt me that a'thing that floats up the North Sea eventually huds up on Aiberdeen beach, right oot in front o' the Inversnecky. So hopefully this will ana'. But please let me ken if you dinna get it.

I'm writing this fae a foxhole, underneath a tunk. No, nae as in airin' cupboard.

It's a bittie nippit; but it's safe fae the bazookas. We're getting' bombarded the hale time by the Huns. And we're naewye near Ibrox.

It's affa dangerous oot on the beach itsel'. Even wi' sunblock. My pal the bricklayer, Cementy Cedric, nearly got mortared. They say life expectancy oot in the open is aboot three minutes. They're nae kiddin'. Yesterday a friendly shell blew up my sandcastle. And I nearly drapped my ice cream cone.

The Nazzies his great big guns, ca'd Wurlitzers. They can fire a three-and-a-half inch shell mair than 5 mile. Or, according to continental units of measurement, an 88 millimetre shell, hindey oot.

The ither day, my tennis partner, Sandy Murray, tried to hit een back wi' his racquet. Fifteen - love.

We've been getting' a richt erse-kicking fae the Jerries, though. Mind you, it's aye a disaster fan ye ging behind awa' fae hame. Spickin' a' hame, we're supposed ti be getting excavated aff the beach. Aye – that'll be richt. There's aboot twa hunner thousand o' us here. It's like Aiberdeen beach. Durin' a door-ti-door collection. I hope they hiv enough pedalos. If it wisna for a' the barrage balloons, we'd get machine gunned by a' the Fokkers. In their Messerschmitts. Spicking a' balloons, fit came o' the cooncil by-elections?

Did you get the brie cheese I sent last month? I hope you wis able ti get it oot the Dazzle bottle. It's nae a patch on Dairylea, but it's rare wi' a Simmers butter biscuit.

I'm nae a big fan a' French food, though. Or as they ca' it, "coos' een". It's a' garlic and ingins. Gads.

They've nae idea fit stovies is. You canna get a decent mock chop supper onywye. A'thing his ti hae some funcy sass. They've nivver even heard a' Bisto. Even though a' their cafes is ca'd "Bistos". Their roast beef's still reed in the middle. And they dinna even bother ti cook their mince. I hid cock-a-leekie soup the ither day. It wis steen cal'.

They div mak a' their ain breed. Nae quite up ti the standard o' a Sunblest. I div like their crescent rolls, though. Or as the French ca' them, "baps". They're like a puffed up rowie, but nae quite as healthy.

They a' drink reed wine here. It's a bittie like Ribena, but you dinna hae to dilute it. It's made oot a foostie grapes, so you widna like it, nae wi your yeast infections. They squash the grapes wi' their feet. But they usually tak aff their sheen first.

I'm thinking a' takkin' a selection back, ti sell ti local bars. Aye, wi' customized labels. E.g. Murdo's Merlot. The Blue Lamp Green Ache. Sorry, Grenache. The Caberfeidh Cabernet. And the Cafe Bardot Bordeaux. Spicking a fit, my ither pal, Hughie, ended up wi' sickness and diarrhoea, a' o'er the heids a' bad wine. He wis up a' night. Chateauneuf ... ti fill a bucket.

By the way, very much obliged for a' the stuff you sent.

I only received one of the flip flops. I gid it to that boy fae Cove. That stood on a mine. It's a shame it wis the wrang fit. So he his ti weer it upsides doon. Underneath his sock.

Thank you for sending my shell collection. That's two shell collections I've got now.

Unfortunately, my egg collection didna survive. I tell a lie – there wis a beak.

I wis affa pleased wi the jigsa' puzzle. Is there ony chunce you could send the lid?

Onywye, I better close now, in case the tunk starts up. You ken I'm easy depressed.

Your loving man,
Barnes ... Noble

Introduction – the present day

Front of Tabs

[Music: Doricula Theme]
(Enter Reverend, carrying a Bible)

Reverend: Dearly beloved … Hullo. What like? I think everybody knows me from the 'Doctor Fa' adventures, but in case not, I'm the Right Reverend Deverend Vale, DD – Oxon; and M Litt – RGU. Minister of St. Machar's cathedral. This evening I'm delighted to introduce the Maggieknockater Thespians and their new Gothic Horror Play, 'Doricula'.

Doricula was adapted by Michael Jamieson (MBChB, Ordinary, Foresterhill); from the 1897 epistolary novel by the Irishman, Abraham - or, as we all know him – Bam Stoker.

Offstage Voice: Fit dis epistolary mean?

Reverend: It means it had a lot a letters in it.

Offstage Voice: Fit, as opposed to numbers?

Reverend: No, not alphabetical letters. Well, it has them, of course. No - letters as in requiring a stamp. Epistles. As in the Apostles of Paul the Epistle. Ha, ha. I do like a little biblical humour.

Now, I don't know if you follow supernatural beings from the halls of fiction. I certainly don't. I only have time for the Lord's good Word (pats his Bible).

But I do believe, nowadays, we don't read nearly enough. There's far too much texting. Our children are growing up inarticulate. As is Mrs Deverend Vale, since she had baith hips removed.

Speaking of horror stories, and bats, Mrs. Deverend Vale gives her apologies. After seeing that Kim Kardashian article in the Sunday Post, she's in having liposuction the night. Aye nae her taes. Her eyelid. Yes, I'm afraid she only has the one eyelid. After that unfortunate accident with the curling iron; when her glass eye melted. Turned oot it was a plastic eye. That would never have happened with BUPA.

All right. Without dropping a "spiler", I can reveal that the legend of the Vampire didn't start in the mountains of central Romania. No, not Cruden Bay, either. It started here, in Aberdeen. 700 years ago.

4

Our play – more of a docudrama, actually, because it's all true - begins in Aberdeen in the present day, then transports us back to 1938, as the Second World War darkly looms. The action, for want of a better word, moves to Transylvania, then back to Aberdeen in 1940, and ends in the present day. After last night's performance the Press and Journal wrote a glowing review. Let me see. (Holds up a newspaper) Here we go. Alistair Selbie. "I've seen worse".

On a more serious note, Doricula is dedicated to our good friend Charles Barron, who left us long before his time, on the 28th of April, 2012; to his lovely wife Gina and their sons, Charlie and Peter. Charles was a gentleman, who inspired and mentored many of us, and who – had he survived - might well have been standing in my place tonight. Thank you, Charles. We all miss you.

Now, let us not forget those most wonderful of virtues, charity and forgiveness. As we heard in Ephesians 4:32 "Be kind to one another, tenderhearted, forgiving one another, as God in Christ forgave you". Although if I find the boy that took the twenty oot the collection plate, he's getting a kick in the hole.

And finally, before we get to the play, let us all sing my favorite, psalm 139 – "Were I to cross from Land to Land, and sail afar by sea: descend the depths or climb the heights …". (Distracted by an unheard voice from offstage) What's that? The organ's been chored? And set alight? In the Asda car park? Bloody casuals. Somebody should droon the parents.

So, with no more ado – Aberdeen, earlier today. The bakery counter at Morrison's.

Chapter 1 - This afternoon.

The Bakery Counter at Morrison's.

[Music: Canned supermarket music]

Announcer: (Over PA. Sing-song over-enthusiastic nasal radio voice. Like a male Gillian Fraser[1]) Hello, Morrison's shoppers! Today's special, in aisle fourteen: free tatties ...

[Sound effect: Crowds running. Screaming. Breaking glass]

Announcer: (Over PA). Clean up on aisle fourteen! Ca' for an ambulance!

(Old Cheryl and Old Clint, pushing shopping carts, bump heavily into each other).

[Sound effect: Carts clanging together]

Cheryl: Hey min! Watch far y'er ga'n! Yi' nearly knocked my pound oot!

Clint: Fit a chick! You bumped into me! Bloody women drivers! Shouldna be allowed oot the hoose. Wait a minute, I ken you!

Cheryl: Oh, I dinna think so.

Clint: Aye I div! Cheryl Noble fae Jasmine Terrace!

Cheryl: No, Wallfield.

Clint: Oh right, Wallfield Noble fae Jasmine Terrace.

Cheryl: No, Cheryl Wallfield.

Clint: Did you get mairied?

Cheryl: Aye.

Clint: Fa till? Wallfield? Far is he? Is he deid?

Cheryl: No, he jist went for tatties. Here he is now.
(Enter Old Wallfield)

---

[1] "Northsound news, Gillian Fraser" c. 1982.

Cheryl: Fit happened?

Wallfield: It wisna free tatties. It wis frittatas. (To Clint) Hello. Fit like?

Clint: Hullo, Wallfield. You dinna look a day over a hundred and twenty nine.

Wallfield: Fit a chick. I'm only a hundred and twenty eight. (To Cheryl) Fa the hell's this?

Cheryl: I dinna ken.

Clint: Div you nae mind? I'm Clint.

Wallfield: Nae Clint Eastneuk...

Cheryl: (Realization dawns) Clint? Is it really you?

Clint: Aye, it's me.

Wallfield: So fit happened? Far hiv you been for the past 73 years?

Clint: It's a lang story ... mind the day the Germans bombed Hall Russell's?

Cheryl: I mind that day – Friday, July 12 1940.

Wallfield: How div you mind that date?

Cheryl: I hiv a perfect memory. I mind fan President Kennedy got stabbed. Like it wis yesterday.

Clint: That wis 1963.

Cheryl: I ken that! No, July 12 wis the day we wis meant to get engaged.

Wallfield: We did get engaged.

Cheryl: No, Clint and me. You and me got engaged the next day.

Clint: You didna hing aboot.

Cheryl: Well, you wis deid, and there wis a war on.

Wallfield: Aye, World War Eye Eye.

Cheryl: You'll hae ti excuse Wallfield – he's dottled.

Wallfield: I'm nae dottled. I got a heid injury in the war.

Clint: Far aboot?

Wallfield: The heid.

Clint: No, I mean, far aboot, geographically. Frunce?

Cheryl: No. The Malt Mill. He fell aff the bar. He nearly knocked o'er my champagne.

Wallfield: The Malt Mill hid champagne, in the war?

Cheryl: It wisna actual champagne. It wis Sangs' Lemonade wi' a grape.

Wallfield: It wisna Sangs' Lemonade.

Cheryl: Fit wis it?

Wallfield: Bon-Accord.

Clint: So far did you bide?

Wallfield: Burnieboozle. Wi' my ma and da.

Clint: I thought that wis jist one-bedroom flats.

Wallfield: Aye, it wis.

Clint: Cosy.

Wallfield: It wisna bad. We hid a double bed. Plus we hid a bomb shelter.

Clint: Fit wye did you hide it?

Wallfield: No, nae 'hid' een – 'hid' een.

Clint: Did you get bombed?

Wallfield: Nearly. There wis a German torch fell doon the lum. It blew up the fire place.

Clint: Far did it come fae?

Wallfield: Archibald's.

Clint: Nae the fireplace. The German torch.

Wallfield: Germany.

Clint: No, far wis it right afore it fell doon the lum?

Wallfield: It wis drapped fae a Stuka.

Clint: Fit, instead o' a bomb?

Wallfield: Maybe it wis an experimental bomb.

Clint: That disna mak ony sense. Wis it on?

Wallfield: The torch?

Clint: No, the fire.

Wallfield: No, there wis nae coal.

Clint: That wis lucky.

Wallfield: Fit's lucky aboot nae haein' coal?

Clint: Lucky the fire wisna on.

Wallfield: Nae really. We'd jist hid the lum swept.

Clint: Why wid you sweep the lum if there wis nae coal?

Wallfield: My da' wis a sweep.

Clint: Did you mak it doon ti the bomb shelter?

Wallfield: Up.

Clint: Fit wye, up? Wis yer bomb shelter in the bedroom?

Wallfield: Hardly. No, it wis in the loft.

Clint: The loft? Fit, in case a bomb drapped up through the fleer?

Wallfield: It wis for bouncin' bombs.

Clint: It wis us that hid the bouncin' bombs.

Wallfield: You hid bombs?

Clint: Nae me - Britain.

Wallfield: It wisna jist the bombs. My da wis feart a' bein' trapped.

Clint: I thought he wis a sweep.

Wallfield: He wisna a good sweep. But he wis a lover. Of music.

Clint: Fit's that got ti dee wi' it?

Wallfield: A' his 78s wis in the loft.

Clint: Oh, that wis very handy.

Wallfield: It wid have been handier if we'd hid a ladder. Or a record player.

Clint: (to Cheryl). Fit aboot you?

Cheryl: Fit aboot me?

Clint: Did you get bombed?

Cheryl: Aye. We hid a bomb fell in the closie. In Jasmine Terrace.

Wallfield: Did it bla' up?

Cheryl: Nae until it exploded. My da' got blown through the windi.

Wallfield: Fit, fae the greenie?

Cheryl: Aye.

Wallfield: Wis he badly hurt?

Cheryl: No, _he_ wisna. But next door's bidey-in wis. Fan my ma found oot.

Wallfield: So fit happened to you? We thought you wis deid.

Clint: I wisna.

Wallfield: Wis you nae?

Clint: No, I wisna.

Wallfield: Did you leave Aiberdeen?

Clint: Aye. I found oot you two got engaged. So I signed up.

Cheryl: You jined the Army?

Clint: No, the circus.

Cheryl: Fit, as a clown?

Clint: How did you guess?

Cheryl: Fit wis your name?

Clint: Clint the Clown.

Cheryl: That's it?

Clint: Aye. Coco wis teen.

Cheryl: You're nae still a clown.

Clint: Aye I am. I jist dinna dee bare-back riding now.

Cheryl: Did yi fa aff?

Clint: No, I got shingles.

Wallfield: Listen you two – how aboot we ging back ti the hoose and catch up o'er a cup a tea and a rowie[2]?

Clint: I dinna ken – I hiv to terrify babies at the Sick Kids later.

Cheryl: Oh come on – Wallfield'll tell you aboot fit happened ti Coont Doricula.

Clint: Coont Doricula? Oh, aye – I never found oot fit happened aboot him. I forgot a' aboot a' that.

Cheryl: He nearly turned me inta a mummy. Luckily, I teen precautions.

Wallfield: Fit precautions?

Cheryl: I kept mi' dra'ers on.

Wallfield: OK, that's enough o' that. Hey, div you mind fan I won you two a trip to Europe?

Clint: Oh, aye. That's far it a' started …

Wallfield: Come on then. I'm parked right oot front.

Clint: In handicapped?

---

[2] The Aberdeen rowie, morning roll or buttery is a staple of northeast cuisine. Other northeast staples include deep-fried rowies, and chicken tikka masala. Misleading in its simplicity, the rowie can't be cooked properly outside of a small number of Aberdeen bakeries (none of which supply Tesco's or Sainsbury's). According to Graeme Thain (of Thain's Bakery fame), most Aberdonians incorrectly think Aitken's rowies are the best. Half of them think it's pronounced "Aikens". Rowies sustained Armstrong, Aldrin and Collins during the 1969 Apollo XI mission to Mars. A rowie was meant to have been planted next to the Star-Spangled Banner for posterity, but Armstrong accidentally ate it. The world record for eating rowies in a single sitting is six (seven would mean forking oot for another bag). The Northeast is evenly divided into people who div, or dinna, scrape the black bitties aff a brunt rowie into the sink, and still eat it (even if the knife maks an affa mess o' the butter). A generation remembers buying rowies in the early seventies from the Chapel Street bakery, en route home from the Palace on a Sunday morning, to save money on a taxi. According to legend, one foursome bought and ate uncooked mince pie crusts because the rowies weren't baked yet. They weren'a affa fine.

Wallfield: Aye.

Clint: You get a handicapped space for being dottled?

Wallfield: No, I jist telt them she's obese.

Cheryl: Fit a bloody chick. I'm nae obese. I hiv a petite figure.

Wallfield: Y'er fat.

Cheryl: Come on, afore I gie him a right handicap.

(They start to exit, pushing the cart)

Wallfield: (Listening to Cheryl whisper something. His voice gets quieter as they exit) Fit wis the doctor ca'd again? Oh aye! Kingseat. It's a' coming back ti' me now ...

[Music: Glittery 'all coming back to me now' chimes]

Chapter 2 - December 22, 1938.

Disastermind Set.

[Music: 'Mastermind' Theme © British Broadcasting Corporation (BBC)]
[Sound Effect: (Music continues) Audience applause. Both fade]

Wallfield is sitting in a chair, spotlight on him. Donnie J Macleodmouth sits opposite him, less harshly lit. He is holding a deck of question cards. Donnie begins in, and occasionally drops into, the northeast vernacular, but tries to maintain a cultured Grampian TV accent.

Donnie: Good evening. And welcome to the very first episode of Grampian TV's weekly Quiz Show, Disastermind. Coming to you live from the Tivoli. Thursday, the 22nd of December, 1938. I'm your quizmaster, Donnie J Macleodmouth. And welcome to our first contestant. What's your name?

Wallfield: Wallfield.

Donnie: Is that your first name or your second?

Wallfield: Baith.

Donnie: And your occupation?

Wallfield: Solicitor. Slash, Real Estate Agent. Slash, Leasing Agent. Slash, Notary Public.

Donnie: I'll just put down 3 slashes.

Wallfield: Slash, Proctor.

Donnie: You mean, "Factor"?

Wallfield: No, proctor. I'm also an inventor.

Donnie: What have you invented?

Wallfield: Heaps a' things. The mobile phone. It wis a disaster. The wheels kept fa'in aff. I hid high hopes for my flameless matches, though.

Donnie: Let me guess. They wouldn't light?

Wallfield: You couldna tell.

Donnie: Well, that's all very interesting, but let's press on. What's your chosen specialist subject?

Wallfield: I hinna decided. It's either the life and times of Benny Yorston - 1927 to 1931 ...

Donnie: Who's Bennie Yorston?

Wallfield: Pass. Ha, ha – jist kidding. He's a fitba player. He played for the Dons.

Donnie: Well, I'm sorry. That's far too specialized a subject. What's your other chosen specialist subject?

Wallfield: Eh, General Knowledge. Let's ging wi' General Knowledge.

Donnie: Your questions on General Knowledge begin - now. How many times did Benny Yorston play for Scotland?

Wallfield: It wis either a hunner or a hunner and one.

Donnie: I must insist on one of them.

Wallfield: Eh, I'll say a hunner.

Donnie: It was one.

Wallfield: Close.

Donnie: What was the one thing Benny Yorston would never do?

Wallfield: Pass.

Donnie: Correct. Benny Yorston holds Aberdeen's club record for scoring how many goals in a season?

Wallfield: A' o' them.

Donnie: Correct. Which scandal is alleged to have ended Benny Yorston's career at Pittodrie?

Wallfield: Stealing a pie.

Donnie: No, two pies.

Wallfield: Wait a minute. I didna choose Benny Yorston. I chose General Knowledge.

Donnie: Everything's General Knowledge. (Examines the question cards). Wait, the cards aren't shuffled properly. I'll shuffle them again (He shuffles the cards). OK. Here we go. How many times did Benny Yorston play for Scotland?

Wallfield: Once?

Donnie: Correct.

Wallfield: Ask me about history or something.

Donnie: Here's a history one. Which team did Benny Yorston play for before Aberdeen?

Wallfield: Mugiemoss.

Donnie: No, Montrose.

Wallfield: Wid you stop asking me aboot Benny Yorston?

Donnie: OK. In 125 BC, which Roman general was the first to defeat the Ligurians?

Wallfield: Could yi ask me aboot Benny Yorston?

Donnie: Oh, come on, just name a famous ancient Roman.

Wallfield: The Pope.

Donnie: No, an army general.

Wallfield: I dinna ken ony Roman generals.

Donnie: Just make up a name.

Wallfield: A' right. Quintus Fulvius Flaccus.

Donnie: Close. Marcus Fulvius Flaccus.

Wallfield: Ask me aboot something else.

Donnie: What is the highest rank in the British Army?

Wallfield: That's easy. General.

Donnie: Field Marshall.

Wallfield: Wid you stop jist asking aboot Generals?

Donnie: That wasn't about Generals. That was about Field Marshalls.

Wallfield: Ask me aboot geology. I ken a' aboot maps.

Donnie: OK. Where about is Eastern Europe?

Wallfield: Right next to Western Europe.

Donnie: Correct. Far wid you find the Azores?

Wallfield: Eyesores? A oe'r Aiberdeen.

Donnie: No, Azores.

Wallfield: The Atlantic Ocean.

Donnie: Could you be more specific?

Wallfield: The Specific Ocean?

Donnie: I'll give you the Atlantic Ocean. What does the female anopheles mosquito transmit?

Wallfield: Oh, a hale host a' diseases.

Donnie: Name one.

Wallfield: I dinna ken ony mosquitoes.

Donny: Name a disease.

Wallfield: Emphysema.

Donny: Name a disease transmitted by mosquitoes.

Wallfield: Jandies.

Donnie: Correct. What do the initials 'TB' stand for?

Wallfield: TB.

Donnie: Correct. Embryology is the study of what?

Wallfield: Folk fae Embra?

Donnie: No, embryos.

Wallfield: Aye, folk fae Embra.

Donnie: What does the urinary bladder contain?

Wallfield: Pash.

[Sound effect: Poopoo poo poo (a la Mastermind)]

Donnie: Mr. Wallfield, your time is up. You answered seven questions correctly. You passed on one. The urinary bladder contains … pish.

Wallfield: That's fit I said.

Donnie: I'm sorry, I can't accept that. And now our next contestant … excuse me a second (holds his hand to his ear, looks around). What, naebody else turned up? That's just brilliant, that. OK, so you're the winner.

Wallfield: Fit rare! Fit's the prize?

Donnie: A season ticket to Pittodrie. 1927 to 1931.

Wallfield: I've already got een.

Donnie: I was kidding. It's two weeks in Eastern Europe! For two! In a famous castle!

Wallfield: Startin' fan?

Donnie: Hogmanay!

Wallfield: That's a crap prize!

Donnie: It's a good prize.

Wallfield: No, it's nae. I dinna hae onybody to invite. And I'm already ga'n ti Eastern Europe for Hogmanay.

Donnie: Well, donate it to a friend.

Wallfield: I suppose. Dis it include getting there?

Donnie: Hardly. It's Grampian TV.

Wallfield: Far aboot is it?

Donnie: Fountainhall Road.

Wallfield: Nae far Grumpian TV is.

Donnie: Oh. Transylvania.

Wallfield: That's far I'm ga'n! I'm meeting a doctor that bides in a castle. He's buyin' een here.

Donnie: Doctor fa?

Wallfield: No, Doctor Acula. I think he specializes in bleed.

Donnie: That's him! It's his castle. Bran Castle. Which other castle is he buying?

Wallfield: Slains.

Donnie: It's ruined.

Wallfield: No, it's square. Oh. He disna care if it's ruined. He's ga'n ti bide in the cellar.

Donnie: So who's getting the trip?

Wallfield: My pal, Clint. Clint Eastneuk. And his bit a' stuff.

Donnie: Who's his bit a' stuff?

Wallfield: Cheryl. Cheryl Noble. They're gettin' engaged. I've never met her.

Donnie: Would you like me to give Mr. Eastneuk the good news?

Wallfield: No, I'll gie him a bell. I'll say it's an engagement present. So, div I get ti come back next wik?

Donnie: I thought you were going to Transylvania next week.

Wallfield: Oh right. But it's only for a few days. Tell you fit, I'll come back on, the following wik.

Donnie: No, we're celebrities every other week. Lewis Grassic Gibbon is on next week.

Wallfield: Is he nae deid?

Donnie: Pass.

[Music: Original Mastermind Theme]

Chapter 3 - December 31, 1938. Late Evening.

Bran Castle[3], Transylvania.

Deep in its bowels. Coffin on the floor.

[Music: Vampire music]

[Sound effect: Coffin lid]

Doricula sits up, makes a gummy face, retrieves his teeth from a tumbler, and inserts them.

Doricula: Ken ess? I've been in this coffin for six hundred and twenty four years. Nae a soul ti spick ti. Ken ess, wi' a lesser person, the strain could have been too much, and they could jist have snapped. Div yi' think so? Aye I div. I'm sorry – I didna introduce mysel'. I'm Wladislaus Dragwlya, but a' my pals ca' me Vlad. Aye, a' my pals at the Vlads' Club! You'd ken me better as Coont Doricula. You maybe ken my feel brither, Coont Backwards. By the way, hiv you heard aboot the dyslexic Vampire? It turned inti a bap. Spickin' a baps - far's Wallfield? Wallfield! Far are yi?!

(Enter Wallfield)

Wallfield: A'right, a'right. Keep your teeth in. Fit's i' maiter?

Doricula: Far's my breakfast?

Wallfield: Fit di your last servant die fae? Onywye, fa the hell his breakfast at night?

Doricula: (gives him a look) ...

Wallfield: Oh, right. Fit div you want for your breakfast?

---

[3] (the following borrows from Wikipedia - http://en.wikipedia.org/wiki/Bran_Castle). Bran Castle, on the border between Transylvania and Wallachia, is commonly known as "Doricula's Castle". There is no evidence that Bam Stoker had even heard of Bran Castle, which has only an indirect association with Vlad III (Voivode (Warlord) of Wallachia), the inspiration for Doricula. Bran is only one of several castles linked to the Doricula legend, including Poenari, Hunyad, Neuschwanstein, and the Salvation Army Citadel.

Doricula: The usual.

Wallfield: A black pudding?

Doricula: Aye, and a Bloody Mary.

Wallfield: Spicy?

Doricula: No! That last een wis o'er spicy. I nearly died ...

Wallfield: Am I deid?

Doricula: No, you're semi-undeid.

Wallfield: Am I a zombie?

Doricula: No, they're deid. You're an apprentice Vampire.

Wallfield: How did I become an apprentice Vampire?

Doricula: I bit your neck. Div you mind?

Wallfield: Of course I mind. I dinna like getting my neck bitten.

Doricula: I mean, do you remember?

Wallfield: Aye. I hiv a photographic memory. I jist dinna hae a camera. Spicking a' cameras, hiv yi heard aboot the constipated photographer?

Doricula: Fit aboot him?

Wallfield: He hid affa polaroids.

Doricula: Div you mind fa I am?

Wallfield: The Penguin?

Doricula: Doricula.

Wallfield: The Vampire?

Doricula: Correct. Div you nae mind knocking at the door last wik?

Wallfield: Oh no. DInna tell me I'm a Mormon[4].

Doricula: Worse.

Wallfield: Nae a Jehovah's Witness.

Doricula: Worse – a solicitor.

Wallfield: Oh, it's a coming back now. I'm wi' Aiberdeen-Considine. And I needed you ti sign a lease, on a hoose.

Doricula: Nae a hoose. A castle. Slains Castle.

Wallfield: At's right. That's far thon boy wrote thon book.

Doricula: Fit book?

Wallfield: Frankenstein.

Doricula: That wis Mary Shelley. Spickin a' fit; far's my Bloody Mary?

Wallfield: Oh, right (exits).

Doricula: Ken ess? I just love a Bloody Mary. I hiv ti hae a Blood Mary to get started in the evening.

(Enter Wallfield with breakfast tray. No Bloody Mary). Far's the Bloody Mary?

Wallfield: We're oot a tomata juice.

---

[4] Mormons and Jehovah's Witnesses have a fundamental characteristic in common – they seriously believe that rubbish. The Aberdeen branch of The Church of Jesus Christ of Latter-Day Saints is one of five Scottish Mormon 'Stakes' (seriously). Mormon missionaries are well-spoken, creepy American loons, always in pairs, in grey suits, chapping on doors in Mastrick and Summerhill, wondering why a'body is aye oot. The Prudential mannie from the 1960s could have wised them up. Jehovah's witnesses are a bigger joke. They're like Mormons, except – according to one who accosted me in Union Street in 1971 – they have briefcases. Seventh Day Adventists are another bunch of clowns, who refuse to lift a finger after dark on Fridays. Accordingly they are unemployable in Medicine (except dermatology), at the Blue Chip or the Co-opy baker; and they hiv nae luck trapping.

Doricula: Fa pits tomata juice in a Bloody Mary? Never mind. Listen, hiv you booked the boat ti' Aiberdeen?

Wallfield: Aye. Two tickets for the morn', January 1st, 1939. The Saint Cluj.

Doricula: Good, I'm looking forward ti' a few years a' peace and quiet. It'll be nice ti' ging back.

Wallfield: Back?

Doricula: Aye. I used ti bide in Aiberdeen.

Wallfield: Far aboot?

Doricula: Countesswells Road.

Wallfield: I bade in Craigiebuckler. Fan wis you there?

Doricula: Oh, about 1314 ...

Wallfield: 13, 14 years ago? We wis neighbours!

Doricula: No, 1314. I fought wi' Robert the Bruce.

Wallfield: At Bannockburn?

Doricula: No, at Peep-Peep's. He knocked o'er my pint.

Wallfield: Did he get you anither een?

Doricula: No, he wis skint. But he gid me a bit a land.

Wallfield: Far aboot?

Doricula: It wis ca'd the Forest a' Stocket. It wis a swump. Turned oot ti be worthless.

Wallfield: Worthless? That's Midstocket. It's worth a fortune!

Doricula: How wid you ken?

Wallfield: I telt yi, I'm a solicitor.

Doricula: Hmm. Interesting. He also gid me an IOU.

Wallfield: How much fur?

Doricula: It wisna fur, it wis dosh. A hundred and twenty million groats.

Wallfield: Groats? Far are they?

Doricula: The Clydesdale Bank.

Wallfield: Queen's Cross?

Doricula: Dinna be feel. There wisna a Queen's Cross. I pit them into Greenfern Road.

Wallfield: Into your Switch?

Doricula: No, my 'Common Good' account. I dinna ken fit's left. They never send a statement.

Wallfield: I ken. And try spicking ti customer service.

Doricula: I ken - you jist get a menu. Can you find out how much is actually in it?

Wallfield: Aye, I've got a pal at the Clydesdale. I'll gie him a shout.

Doricula: I hope naebody's interfered wi' it.

Wallfield: How d'you mean interfered?

Doricula: Spent it on some hair-brained scheme.

Wallfield: Fit – like filling Union Terrace Gardens wi' cement?

Doricula: Aye. Or building an Art Gallery far you canna park.

Wallfield: So how come you left Aiberdeen?

Doricula: I got killed.

Wallfield: Aye. Peep-Peep's is rough.

Doricula: No, at the Forest of Stocket.

Wallfield: Oh. Did a tree fa' on yi?

Doricula: No, I got killed wi' a werewolf.

Wallfield: Is that why you're 700 years al'... and sleep in a coffin... and never ging oot during the day? Are you Helen St. Mirren?

Doricula: No, a Vampire.

Wallfield: How come you didna get beeried there in the swump.

Doricula: I did. But I kept floatin' up.

Wallfield: Fit's it like being a Vampire?

Doricula: It sucks. You hiv ti work nights.

Wallfield: Div you really hiv ti drink blood ti survive?

Doricula: Aye.

Wallfield: Spickin' a blood, guess fit my motto is.

Doricula: "Be positive".

Wallfield: No, "Be prepared".

Doricula: Wis you a Boy Scout?

Wallfield: No, a BB. Is it true you canna stand garlic?

Doricula: I love garlic. I just dinna like pasta.

Wallfield: Is it true you hinna got a reflection?

Doricula: Aye.

Wallfield: So how div you shave?

Doricula: Because I'd look stupid wi' a beard. Ony mair questions?

Wallfield: Is it true sunlight wid kill yi?

Doricula: Aye. But it dis wonders for my psoriasis. No, there's only one thing that kills me.

Wallfield: A stake?

Doricula: Aye, if I choked on een. Ha, ha. No, it's haein' my heart cut oot and burned and my heid cut aff and beeried in holy ground.

Wallfield: So if a piana fell on your heid, you'd be a'right?

Doricula: No – that ana'. That's enough aboot killing me. G'wan pack my coffin for the trip ti Aiberdeen. Mak sure it's got plenty a' fresh dubs in it. But nae worms this time. And nae toldies. We're leaving at first light. OK - I'm ga'n oot.

Wallfield: First fittin'?

Doricula: No, I'm ga'n oot for one last feed.

Wallfield: Fit, you're ga'n to satisfy yoursel' on the bleed o' some unsuspecting young virgin?

Doricula: No. I'm ga'n for a kebab. (He exits)

Chapter 4 - December 31, 1938. Almost midnight.

A stage coach bouncing through Transylvania at night.

[Sound effect: Coach Wheels]
[Sound effect: Thunder]
[Sound effect: Horses whinny]

Cheryl and Clint sit side by side, both bouncing all over the place. Clint is pouring wine & spilling it.

Cheryl: Clint! Ye'r getting wine a' oe'r my clies!

Clint: Nae problem, Cheryl. I've got reed wine ana' – that'll get the stains oot.

Cheryl: You're nae wise.

Clint: I am sut wise. Is this nae romantic?

Cheryl: Romantic? Fit? Bouncing aroon in a stagecoach in the middle o' the night?

Clint: It's nae the middle o' the night. It's quarter ti midnight.

Cheryl: I still dinna ken why we hid to come ti Romania for Hogmanay.

Clint: Yiv aye said you fancied ga'n ti Transylvania.

Cheryl: I said "Pennsylvania".

Clint: Oh. Serves you right for mumbling.

Cheryl: You're aye takin' me on crap holidays.

Clint: No, I'm nae.

Cheryl: Fit about thon rowing holiday?

Clint: Rowing's healthy.

Cheryl: Nae fan it's across the Atlantic.

Clint: That wis a once in a lifetime experience.

Cheryl: Aye – naebody else his ever rowed inti an iceberg.

Clint: You wis the een rowin'.

Cheryl: You wis the een steerin'.

Clint: It wisna my fault. It wis dark. Plus I hid ti swerve for thon big boat. Fit wis it ca'd?

Cheryl: The Titanic. And it wis them that hid ti swerve for us.

Clint: Well, it wis nice of them to send doon a lifeboat. Even if they didna mean ti'.

Cheryl: Too bad it had a hole in it.

Clint: Fit, the lifeboat?

Cheryl: No, the Titanic.

Clint: That wisna my fault either.

Cheryl: Aye it wis. If you hidna distracted them, they widna have hit the same iceberg.

Clint: It wisna me that distracted them. It was a' the fireworks they wis settin' aff. They're lucky the boat didna catch fire. I'm surprised they even noticed us.

Cheryl: Well, it wis nice o' them ti winch us up.

Clint: Aye. Although a cup a' tea would have been nice. Nivver mind a Jammie Dodger.

Cheryl: Well, they wis busy. Wi' that lifeboat drill.

Clint: I wisna impressed by the hale shebang.

Cheryl: Fit wye nae?

Clint: Well, it wis supposed ti be a luxury liner. But it wis a' weet inside. Plus it wis on a slope. And nae jist that.

Cheryl: Fit?

Clint: The band wis playing ootside.

Cheryl: Fit wis wrang wi' that?

Clint: It wis freezing cal'. Plus you couldna hear them o'er the horn. And I wisna impressed wi the music selection.

Cheryl: Fit, 'Nearer My God to Thee'?

Clint: Aye. Fan I'd requested 'Roamin' in the Gloamin'.

Cheryl: Still, that wis nae excuse ti steal the lifeboat.

Clint: Fit wye nae? They hid heaps o' them. Plus they still hinna reimbursed me for the canoe. I'd ca' that fair's fair.

Cheryl: Some lifeboat. It couped.

Clint: That wis a' the folk hinging onto the side. Well, it could have turned oot worse.

Cheryl: Worse? I lost my handbag. And a shoe.

Clint: Why wis your shoes in your handbag?

Cheryl: They wisna in my handbag. They wis in my pooch.

Clint: Oh, stop complaining. It wis 26 years ago.

Cheryl: I've still got chilblains. Fit aboot last year, then?

Clint: Fit aboot it? You said you'd love ti ging up in a balloon.

Cheryl: Aye. But nae the Hindenburg.

Clint: I ken. I feel bad. Div you think we should of sut in smoking?

Cheryl: I telt you it was stupid ti try oot a flamethrower in a blimp.

Clint: It wisna a flamethrower. It wis a pizza electric lighter.

Cheryl: Fitever. I telt you a barbecue wis a bad idea.

Clint: We never hid ony trouble wi' the barbecue on the R101.

Cheryl: Aye, 'cause we crashed afore you lit the charcoal.

Clint: Only 'cause it wis weet.

Cheryl: It wis such a terrible waste.

Clint: Fit, the charcoal?

Cheryl: No, nae the charcoal!

Clint: Oh, the drumsticks. It wisna that bad. They wis half price at Lidl's.

[Sound effect: A wolf howls]

Cheryl: Fit wis that?

Clint: Probably a werewolf. They're a' o'er the place.

Cheryl: Clint!! I'm feart! Are we nearly there?

Clint: It's jist roon the corner.

Cheryl: It better be a nice hotel.

Clint: It's nae a hotel. It's a castle.

Cheryl: Oh, fit rare.

Clint: Even mair rare - we hiv the hale castle ti wersels.

Cheryl: Ooh! I've aye fancied haein' my ain butler.

Clint: Eh ... there's nae actually a butler per se. It's nae Doontoon Abbey.

Cheryl: Well, I suppose we could butle wersel's. Fit aboot a cook?

Clint: I wis hoping you'd be the cook.

Cheryl: You ken I dinna cook.

Clint: I ken, but this is your holidays. You can tik a break fae nae cookin'.

Cheryl: Ken ess? I kint you were thick, but I never thought you'd spend good money ti bide in an empty castle.

Clint: I never spent money: it's free!

Cheryl: Free? You cheap so and so. Fa gid it ti yi?

Clint: You ken my pal Wallfield? He won it on Disastermind. He's there right now – he's ga'n ti let us in.

Cheryl: I could go a decent sleep. I'm knackered.

Clint: I thought you got a sleep on the Orient Express.

Cheryl: I didna. I wis soakin'.

Clint: I telt you ti bring a tool for sweemin' the Channel.

Cheryl: I thought you meant a hammer.

Clint: Is that fit wye yi kept sinking?

Cheryl: No, I forgot the hammer. It must have been the golf clubs.

Clint: Well, I hid a leak in my sleeper.

Cheryl: It wisna rainin'.

Clint: I ken. I jist couldna be bothered ga'n ti the lavvie.

Cheryl: Gads! I jist hope this castle's nae hunted.

Clint: They're a' hunted here.

Cheryl: Fit?

Clint: I'm kidding. Y'er ga'n ti love bringing in the New Year at Castle Doricula.

Cheryl: Doricula? The Vampire?

Clint: Aye. But he winna be there. He's takking aff.

Cheryl: I'm nae ga'n ti sleep a wink. Can we stop at a Morrison's on the wye?

Clint: Fit for? Garlic?

Cheryl: No, Valium.

Clint: Too late – we're here.

[Sound effect: Clatter of coach wheels on cobblestones]
[Sound effect: Horses whinny]

Chapter 5 - December 31, 1938. Almost midnight.

Castle Doricula - Front Door.
Sign "Castle Doricula. Nae Minkers Aloud".
(Cheryl is standing at the door. Clint is talking to Arthur Bean, who has a Polish-Doric accent).

Cheryl: Are we there yet?

Clint: Aye, we're there yet. (To Arthur, who is offloading the luggage) Div you tak credit cards?

Arthur: Fit's a credit card?

Clint: I invented them. Well, I invented the magnetic strip.

Arthur: Fit div they dee?

Cheryl: They let your bunk chore your savings.

Clint: That's a slight exaggeration.

Cheryl: Fit wid you ca' it, then?

Clint: Annual fees, service fees, late fees, overdraft fees and interest.

Cheryl: Telt you – chorin'.

Arthur: How div you stop somebody else using it?

Cheryl: You dinna.

Clint: Cut it oot. Aye yi div. That's fit the PIN number's for.

Arthur: Fit's a PIN number?

Clint: It's a Personal Identification Number number.

Arthur: That's unnecessarily redundant, that.

Cheryl: Dinna tell him aboot your ATM Machines.

Clint: Shut up. Fit aboot a check?

Arthur: I dinna trust Czechs.

Clint: I ken. They're too easy to forge.

Arthur: No, they murdered Good King Wenceslas.

Cheryl: Fa?

Arthur: The boy that got hit wi' the sna'ba'.

Cheryl: Fit sna'ba'?

Arthur: (sings) *Good King Wenceslas once looked oot, on the Feast a' Wenceslas. A sna'ba' hit him in the mooth and nearly knocked him senseless.* Far are you fae?

Cheryl: Aiberdeen.

Arthur: Aiberdeen! I bade there! That's far I got my accent!

Clint: Fit accent?

Cheryl: How lang wis you there?

Arthur: Oh, five, six days.

Cheryl: Far did you work? TODA?

Arthur: Claben.

Cheryl: The fish?

Arthur: Aye. They hid an openin', and they asked if I could fillet.

Clint: So, fit's the fare?

Arthur: One million New Loos. Sorry - elevenpence three farthings.

Clint: Fit? That's jist extortion, that. Are you related ti' Hitler?

Arthur: Aye. He's my cousin. We wint ti school the gither.

Cheryl: Far, Austria?

Arthur: No, here. George Coşbuç High School. It's twinned wi' Powis.

Clint: Adolf Hitler's your cousin?

Arthur: No, Dod Hitler.

Clint: Dod?

Arthur: Georgescu, but we ca'd him Dod.

Clint: "Ca'd him"? Is he deid?

Arthur: No, he hid a sex change.

Clint: Fit is he now? Georgia?

Arthur: Dodette. Fa's Adolf Hitler?

Clint: Div you nae ken? The heid boy fae Germany.

Arthur: Oh, right. The boy that's aboot to annex the Sudetenland.

Cheryl: My neighbour jist pit in one o' them.

Clint: Fit?

Cheryl: An annexe.

Clint: I think my neighbour's a German spy. He's aye lookin' in the lavvie windi'.

Cheryl: He's nae a German spy. He's jist a dirty al' mannie.

Clint: How wid you ken?

Cheryl: I'm pals wi' his doather, Sieghilda.

Arthur: Onywye, I dinna hae change.

Clint: Well, this is the sma'est I hiv (holds up a huge 1938 Clydesdale Bank £20 note).

Arthur: Fit, the hell is that? It's huge. A' pink and purple. oh, I ken - the new Scotland awa' strip?

Clint: Shut up. It's a twenty pound note.

Arthur: Fit's this? Clydesdale Bunk? I'm sorry, I dinna accept Australian money.

Clint: Cheryl - hiv you got change? It's elevenpence three farthings.

Cheryl: I've only got a shilling (gives it to him)

Clint: That'll dee (gives it to Arthur). There you are – keep the change.

Arthur: A farthing? Fa are you? Andrew Carnegie?

Clint: Fa, the barber? No, I'm nae. Onywye, you can never say Aiberdonians is grippy. Div you hae a phone? In case we need a ride back.

Arthur: Aye, here it is.

Clint: That's jist a can. Far's the string?

Arthur: There's nae a string. It's a mobile.

Clint: Fit's the number?

Arthur: Here's my business card. Jist gie's a bell.

Clint: Ta. A' right. Let's let Wallfield ken we're here.

Cheryl: Far's the bell?

Clint: Maybe it's this chain.

[Sound effect: toilet flushing]
[Sound effect: Scary echoey footsteps, dragging slowly on a stone floor, approaching]
[Sound effect: Old Heavy Door opens]

Wallfield: Clint! Fit like, min?!

Clint: Oh, nae bad. Chavvin'.

Wallfield: Dinna bide oot there. Come in! And you must be Cheryl. (to Clint) She disna look like a boot.

Cheryl: Fit?!! You said I wis a boot?

Clint: No! I said you wis aboot forty.

Wallfield: Oh, sorry! So, Cheryl - foo you deein?

Cheryl: Nae bad, apart fae a sair erse.

Wallfield: TMI.

Cheryl: No - fae bouncin' up and doon.

Wallfield: Mair TMI.

Cheryl: You must be Wallfield.

Wallfield: That's me. Wallfield Wallfield. But jist ca' me Wallfield.

Cheryl: Is this really Doricula's castle?

Wallfield: It's one o' his castles. He jist bought anither een in Scotland. Slains.

Cheryl: He's nae hame, is he?

Wallfield: Fa?

Cheryl: Doricula.

Wallfield: Oh, I'm sorry – my memory's been affa, lately. I hiv ambrosia.

Cheryl: Amnesia.

Wallfield: No ambrosia. There's 24 tins in the scullery. If you like rice pudding.

Cheryl: So, is he nae at hame?

Wallfield: No, he's nae. Fa?

Cheryl: Doricula!

Wallfield: No, he's oot.

Cheryl: Is he coming back?

Wallfield: Aye – he'll be back afore it gets light.

Clint: Fan dis it get light?

Wallfield: Fan the sun comes up.

Cheryl: (to Clint) Clint! You said the place wid be empty!

Wallfield: It will be – the mor'n. Then I'm takkin' him ti Aiberdeen.

Cheryl: You mean I hiv ti spend a night in a hunted castle wi' a Vampire?

Clint: Oh, we probably winna even see him. He'll probably jist slip inti his coffin.

Cheryl: "Probably winna see him"? I ken fit happens in these stories. The Vampire visits the beautiful virgin in her boudoir.

Wallfield: I think you'll be safe enough

Cheryl: Shut up. I hinna finished. She succumbs ti his charms …

Clint: Sucks fit?

Cheryl: Shut up. I am nae haein' my neck bitten, and a' my bleed drained, and turned inti a Vampire.

Wallfield: Oh, stop it. I can 100% guarantee you winna meet Doricula. Trust me. On my mother's grave.

(Doricula appears from nowhere. He has a Transylvanian vampire accent, with the slightest northeast inflection)

Doricula: Hullo. Did onybody mention mothers' graves?

Cheryl: (screams) Oh, my God!

Clint: I didna ken your mother wis deid.

Wallfield: She's nae. But she's got a plot picked oot.

Clint: Far aboot?

Wallfield: Trinity.

Clint: Oh, that's rare. It's right handy for the Beach End.

Wallfield: And they dinna let jist onybody in.

Clint: I ken. You hiv ti be deid.

Cheryl: That dis it! Clint - I am nae bidin' here! Get me oot a here.

Doricula: Oh, come on. Fit are you feart o'? Nithin's ga'n ti happen. Please – jist one night.

Cheryl: Over my deid body.

Doricula: I'm nae touchin' that wi' a stick.

Cheryl: Clint! Get me oot a here! I am NAE bidin'!

Clint: There's naewye else we could ging, wi' Scottish money.

Wallfield: Actually, there is a place in Cluj that taks Scottish money.

Cheryl: Far?

Wallfield: The Airport Skean Dhu.

Cheryl: (Thinks about it) I suppose we could bide here one night.

Chapter 6 – January 1, 1939. Afternoon.

Castle Doricula - Dining Room.
Clint is sitting at the table. Cheryl stumbles in, still half drunk, unkempt.

Clint: Oh – hullo. Finally. Happy New Year's aifterneen.

Cheryl: There's nae need ti shout.

Clint: I'm nae shouting.

Cheryl: My heed's splittin', and my lugs is dirling. Fit happened?

Clint: Fit, before or aifter you passed oot?

Cheryl: I didna pass oot. I hid a migraine.

Clint: Well, before you passed oot fae y'er migraine, you drunk eight BabyChams, four crème de menthes, and a Pernod.

Cheryl: Oh, my God. A' that on an empty stomach?

Clint: No, that wis afore you ordered in the pizza.

Cheryl: Fit kind a pizza?

Clint: Jam.

Cheryl: Fit kind a jam?

Clint: Robertsons. Oh. Rasps.

Cheryl: Oh, I love rasps. Fit time did I ging ti bed?

Clint: I dinna ken. You wis still unconscious fan I went oot.

Cheryl: Went oot? Fit, for? First fittin'? Far? Fa wi'?

Clint: Me and Wallfield went ti the local. Club Cluj.

Cheryl: "Club Cluj". Fit kind a place is that?

Clint: I think the local Romanian term is 'tittie bar'.

Cheryl: Clint! That's nae your kind a' bar.

Clint: I ken! It's nae my scene. I jist went ti keep Wallfield company.

Cheryl: Wis there nudity?

Clint: I couldna see for the fan.

Cheryl: An Ostrich fan?

Clint: No, a Dons' fan.

Cheryl: Why wis there a Dons' fan?

Clint: They played Cluj in the Europa League.

Cheryl: On Hogmanay?

Clint: No, March.

Cheryl: He's still here?

Clint: He bides here. He's thinkin' a' giein' up his Pittodrie season ticket.

Cheryl: Because he's never there?

Clint: No, because they're shite.

Cheryl: I canna believe you wis ogling ither quines' bodies. A sophisticated quine like me wid never reveal mair than her bunions.

Clint: So how come a' your clies wis doon here fan we got back?

Cheryl: Fit? Oh my God. I dinna mind. I wis blootered.

Clint: It must have been Doricula! He got Wallfield ti get you drunk, and ti get me oot o' the picture, and then he hid his evil wye wi' yi. Let me see your neck. (Cheryl reveals her neck) Look – there's bleed!

Cheryl: That wis jist me shaving.

(Enter Doricula, also unkempt; holding his head and the side of his neck, followed by Wallfield, also holding his head)

Doricula: Oh, my heid ... Wallfield – fit hiv you got for a sair heid?

Wallfield: Aspirin.

Doricula: Oh, no – I canna tak aspirin.

Clint: Ulcer?

Doricula: No – thins your bleed.

Clint: (looking closely at Doricula) Fit's that mark on your neck?

Doricula: Yer blonde gid me a love bite.

(Clint is speechless)

Cheryl: Me? Fan?

Doricula: Right after you took aff a' your clies. And right afore you threw up.

Cheryl: I never threw up.

Doricula: Aye you did. There wis seeds. Gads.

Wallfield: I'm nae cleaning it up.

Doricula: It's a'right. The werewolf ate it.

Cheryl: So, you're tellin' me you didna try ti get aff wi' me?

Doricula: Hardly. I'm only interested in young virgins.

Cheryl: Eh, excuse me. I am young. For fifty-two. And a half. I nearly got a trap at the Palace last wik.

Doricula: I'm nae interested in minkers.

Cheryl: Minkers? Fit a chick. Clint – pit the heid on him.

Clint: You wis oot trapping at the Palace? And then you gid a Vampire a love bite?

Cheryl: Aye but I didna hae sex wi' him. Did I?

Doricula: No. You jist gid me two shillings for a lap dance.

Cheryl: I vaguely mind that. Wis you wearing your cloak?

Doricula: No, you wis. And nithing else.

Clint: You wasted two shillings o' our holiday money on a lap dance?

Doricula: Forty two shillings.

Clint: That's it. The engagement's aff!

Cheryl: Fit engagement?

Clint: Oor engagement.

Cheryl: I didna ken we wis engaged. Although it wid be high time …

Clint: "High time"?

Cheryl: Well, we hiv been ga'n oot for thirty eight years

Clint: Dinna exaggerate. Thirty seven. I wis ga'n ti propose ti you last night. But nae now. Awa' you go wi' your new lad.

Cheryl: Come on Clint. It wis jist a momentary drunken lapse. I wis only thinking aboot you.

Clint: I'm nae kidding. I could never be wi' an unfaithful person. I'm ga'n ti pawn the ring. (He looks in his pockets). Wallfield – far's the ring?

Wallfield: You gid it ti the stripper.

(Clint looks guiltily at all)

Clint: I'll tell you fit – we'll ca' it a dra'.

Cheryl: No, we winna ca' it a dra'. You go and get that ring back right now.

Clint: Oh, a'right. Wallfield – are you coming?

Doricula: Hud your horses - I need Wallfield here. We're just about to leave.

Wallfield – get us a coach for the train station. And mind it needs ti be big enough to cairy a coffin.

Wallfield: Is somebody deid? Oh – right.
(Doricula exits)

Cheryl: Clint! Did you hear that?

Clint: Aye. Hear fit?

Cheryl: There's a train station right here in Cluj!

Clint: And?

Cheryl: So how come I hid ti sit on a plunk in a stagecoach for two days fae Bucharest?

Clint: I thought it'd be mair romantic.

Cheryl: Oh Clint ... sometimes you surprise me.

Clint: Plus it wis quarter the price.

(Wallfield picks up ancient phone and dials).

Wallfield: Be quiet you two. I'm ringing. Zero ... zero ... zero ... zero ... zero ... zero ... ... zero.

[Sound effect: Phone rings 3 times & is connected]

Wallfield: Hello? Hello?

Operator: (painfully slow) Hullooo ...

Wallfield: Hello? Operator?

Operator: Hullo ...? This is the operator ... spickin'.

Wallfield: Yes, hello. Coach company, please.

Operator: You wint a cooch?

Wallfield: No, a coach.

Operator: My loon's selling a cooch. Div yi want the cheers?

Wallfield: No, nae a cooch, a coach.

Operator: It's a good een. It's fae the Blind Workshop. Real vinyl.

Wallfield: Would you pit me through ti the coach company? Nae your loon.

Operator: Fit coach company wid you like?

Wallfield: Fit's the choices?

Operator: There's Cluj Coaches, and there's Cluj Executive Coaches.

Wallfield: Gimme Cluj Executive Coaches.

Operator: They closed doon.

Wallfield: OK, pit me through ti Cluj Coaches.

Operator: Please hold ...

[Sound effect: Phone rings 3 times & is connected]

Operator: Hullo? Cluj Coaches here.

Wallfield: Is that still you?

Operator: No, it's nae me. This is Cluj Coaches. Can I help you?

Wallfield: Aye. I need a coach ti the station.

Operator: The train station or the bus station?

Wallfield: Is there a bus station?

Operator: No.

Wallfield: A'right - the train station.

Operator: Please hold.

Wallfield: Fit for?

[Sound effect: Phone rings 3 times & is connected]

Operator: Hullo – Cluj Executive Coaches.

Wallfield: I thought you wis closed doon.

Operator: Fa telt you that?

Wallfield: I need a coach ti the station.

Operator: Fan?

Wallfield: The day.

Operator: We're closed.

Wallfield: The day?

Operator: No, doon.

[Sound effect: Phone hung up]

Cheryl: Ca' Arthur Bean.

Wallfield: Fa?

Cheryl: Oor coach driver.

Wallfield: Fit's his number?

Cheryl: It's on his business card. Here we go ... eh - two.

[Sound effect: Phone receiver ringing in earpiece]

Arthur: Hullo? Arthur Bean and Sons; Executive Coaches.

Wallfield: Aye. Fae Cluj?

Arthur: Fae Bucharest.

Wallfield: Oh, for f... How far is Bucharest fae Cluj?

Arthur: Two days. Plus or minus.

Wallfield: Plus or minus fit?

Arthur: Plus or minus two days.

Wallfield: His Lordship'll jist hae ti wait two days. Is there room for a coffin?

Arthur: Aye. On your lap.

Wallfield: A' right. Jist get here as fast as you can. (Hangs up).

[Sound effect: Same Doorbell]

Wallfield: Fa's that?

(Clint goes to answer the door. Clint re-enters with Arthur).

Wallfield: Arthur Bean?

Arthur: And sons.

Wallfield: You said it wis two days fae Bucharest.

Arthur: Aye, it is. But I wis ootside.

Wallfield: You didna say you wis ootside.

Arthur: You didna ask.

Wallfield: Fit wis you deein' outside?

Arthur: I never left. I took you back fae Club Cluj. Mind?

Wallfield: Vaguely. But that wis last night.

Arthur: Aye, but I've still got your stripper. Or should I say – your fiancée? She said ti wait.

Clint: Is the meter still runnin'?

Arthur: Fit's a meter?

Wallfield: Thirty nine inches.

Clint: Is anither een a' my inventions. It tells you how much the fare is, according to how far you've went, and how long you've teen.

Arthur: I jist mak that up.

Wallfield: I didna ken you wis wi' Comcabs.

Clint: Dis she still hae my ring?

Arthur: Aye. Div you still hae her clies?

Clint: I hinna got her clies.

Arthur: You wis sniffin' her punts fan we left.

Clint: No I wisna. I was bla'in my nose.

Arthur: Gads!

Clint: It wisna her punts.

Cheryl: Well, it wisna mine.

Clint: It wisna onybody's punts. It wis my hunkie.

Arthur: So fit div you want me ti dee wi' her?

Clint: Dee me a favour.

Arthur: Fit?

Clint: (takes out the £20 note again) Tak the twenty. Gie her a shilling and get the ring back. And change. Div you think she his nineteen guineas on her?

Arthur: I'm sure she dis. But it'll a' be thruppennies.

Clint: It wis only thruppence for a lap dance? (To Cheryl) And you gid yer toy boy two shillings!

Arthur: No. Lap dunces wis a ha'peny. It wis thruppence for the VIP room.

Cheryl: My engagement ring wis only a shilling?

Clint: No, that's jist ti get it back.

Cheryl: How much wis it?

Clint: Oh, it wis infinitely mair than that.

Cheryl: How much?

Clint: I widna like ti say. Modesty forbids, ken?

Cheryl: How much?

Clint: Two shillings.

Cheryl: You grippy Raj.

Arthur: Of course, it's nae jist the ring. She's pregnant.

Cheryl: You got a stripper pregnant? In one night?

Clint: How mony nights dis it tak?

Wallfield: Actually, it wis me.

Clint: You? You owe me thruppence, then.

Wallfield: It wisna last night. It wis March. Right aifter the Dons' game. Or it could have been right afore. Or during.

Clint: During?

Wallfield: Aye, it wis a lang line for the pies.

Cheryl: Did you dee the decent thing?

Wallfield: No, I only had enough for one pie.

Cheryl: No - did you mairy her?

Wallfield: I tried. But her brother widna let me.

Cheryl: Why nae?

Wallfield: Their divorce wisna through yet.

Cheryl: (To Clint) You couldna tell your stripper wis nine month's pregnant?

Clint: They a' look nine months pregnant.

Wallfield: Look, jist get rid o' her.

Arthur: Fit, Cheryl?

Wallfield: No, the stripper.

Arthur: Fit stripper?

Wallfield: The een in the coach.

Arthur: There's four in the coach.

Wallfield: The pregnant een.

Arthur: They're a' pregnant.

Wallfield: The een I got pregnant.

Arthur: You got them a' pregnant.

Wallfield: The een wi' the ring.

Arthur: They a' hiv a ring. Somewye.

Wallfield: Engagement.

Arthur: Oh. Fit div you mean, get rid o' her? Kill her?

Wallfield: No! Jist get the ring, tak them a' hame, and come right back.

Arthur: A'right. See yi' later!

(Takes the £20 and exits)

Wallfield: OK, you two. I'm takking the Coont ti' Aiberdeen.

Clint: Why Aiberdeen?

Wallfield: That's far he used ti bide. He wants to claim his property.

Clint: Fit property?

Wallfield: The Common Good Fund.

Clint: He ains the Common Good Fund?

Wallfield: And he ains Midstocket. Robert the Bruce gid them ti' him.

Clint: There canna be much left in the Common Good Fund.

Wallfield: Aye there is.

Clint: How much?

Wallfield: Guess.

Clint: Two quid.

Wallfield: Mair.

Clint: Two guineas.

Wallfield: Fourteen billion quid.

Clint: How div you ken that?

Wallfield: I phoned the Clydesdale Bunk.

Clint: Fourteen Billion? Ken ess? Wi' a' that money, Aiberdeen could be the greatest City on Earth! We could hae an ice rink! We could hae the world's number one and number two pitch and putts. We could hae the best fitba team in Europe! We could beat Real Madrid!

Wallfield: Hardly.

Cheryl: We could hae an Art Gallery, that wisna a' that modrin rubbish. It could be a beautiful Greek building. And then they could pit a huge ugly metal roof on the top of it. Like a B&Q. It could serve overpriced tea and cal' rowies. We could hae wer ain Symphony Orchestra! And an Opera Company! And a Ballet!

Clint: Hud on … let's jist stick wi the ice rink and the fitba team.

Cheryl: No way. I've dreamed aboot a haein' a ballet since I heard aboot the fourteen billion.

Clint: Fit, three seconds ago?

Cheryl: No, I've kent since I wis little. I heard the Lord Provost telling my ma, fan she wis alive.

Clint: Fit een?

Cheryl: I only hid one ma.

Clint: No, fit Provost?

Cheryl: Hazelheid.

Clint: Fit wye wid he tell your ma?

Cheryl: He's my uncle.

Clint: Provost Hazelheid is your uncle? How come he's nae ca'd Noble? Wait a minute. He's nae her brither, is he?

Cheryl: No, my mum wisna ca'd Hazelheid. He's nae really my uncle. Mair like a step uncle. He used ti come o'er a' the time. Fan my da wis oot.

Wallfield: Look, I hiv to ging. You two can bide here as long as you want. But I wouldna bide o'er long.

Cheryl: Fit wye?

Wallfield: You ken thon boy Adolf Hitler?

Cheryl: Aye. Thon coonciller fae Germany?

Wallfield: Chuncellor. Aye, him. He's somewye in the Sudetenland of now.

Cheryl: For his holidays?

Wallfield: No. Wi' his Wehrmacht. He's aboot ti invade the rest a' Czechoslovakia.

Cheryl: That's naewye near here.

Wallfield: Aye, but they're coming here next.

Clint: How far awa are they?

Wallfield: Jist up the road. Six hundred miles.

Clint: That's like fae London ti Aiberdeen. It'll tak them two wiks ti get here.

Wallfield: Aye, but two hoors in a Stuka. Onywye, I'm awa ti pack. How mony keys will you need?

Cheryl: Neen – we're coming wi' you!

Chapter 7 - July 11 1940[5]. Early evening.

A meeting of the Woolmanhillati[6], at Woolmanhill.

Abraham Van Hazelheid is wearing the attire of the Grand Master of the Woolmanhillati.
Indistinct background conversations. It is pitch dark, lit only by an occasional match flare.
Hazelheid: (Taps gavel) Order, order! Let's have order!

---

[5] The evening before the infamous bombing of Hall Russell shipyards, and the shooting down of a Luftwaffe Heinkel He 111H-3 bomber into the new ice skating rink at South Anderson Drive. Ironically, the Heinkel had originally targeted Leuchars airfield, with harbour installations at Broughty Ferry and Dundee, as alternates. Had the Heinkel bombed Dundee, an intact ice rink would certainly have tipped the balance in Aberdeen's 2013 bid to beat Dundee for UK City of Culture 2017. As neither won, many consider it a moot point.

[6] The Woolmanhillati is a well-known secret society founded on May 2nd, 1776, by Captain John 'Mad Jack' Byron, to "tak the piss oot o' the Bavarians" - a vision not finally realized until March 16, 1983. Mad Jack is best known for fathering George Gordon ('Lord') Byron - in turn best known for having one of Aberdeen's most beautiful and popular civic squares named after him. Plus a pub. The Woolmanhillati's original goals were identical to those of the Illuminati – "to oppose superstition, prejudice, religious influence over public life, abuses of state power, and to support women's education and gender equality". At its first board meeting the words "promote" and "oppose" were switched. Membership of the present day Woolmanhillati remains a secret, closely guarded by Aberdeen FC's board and their chums. (Secret societies are universally distrusted, but only by people not in them) The Woolmanhillati have selflessly fostered and continue to foster outstanding civic works, such as the Muse Marischal Square Fiasco (the replacement for St Nicholas House), glass boxes and / or crappy student flats around the Triple Kirks, the Denburn Center, E&M's extensions (the old concrete one and the new one that'll look like an aquarium stuck on the side), the YMCA on Union Street, the Lang Stracht Hotel, the 'Seven Incorporated Trades' building on Holburn Street, and the tourist magnets at Beechwood Court, Castleton Court, Denburn Court, Donside Court, Elphinstone Court, Grandholm Court, Greig Court, King's Court, Linksfield Court, Marischal Court, Northsea Court, Oldcroft Court, Promenade Court, Regent Court, Seamount Court, St Machar Court and Woodhill Court. Notably, none of architects who designed these latter soaring masterpieces ever lived in them, preferring (for unclear reasons) less visionary properties in Sanday Road and Hamilton Place.

Duthie: Pint a' export, please.

Hazelheid: Shut up. Order! Meeting of the holiest and most secret order of the Brothers of Aiberdeen. Thursday July 11, 1940. For the record, I am Grand Master Abraham Van Hazelheid, Heid Bummer o' the Woolmanhillati.

Duthie: Hey, I thought we wis supposed ti be the Illuminati. The enlightened eens.

Hazelheid: Aye, we are. So?

Duthie: If we're a' enlightened, how come it's pitch black?

Hazelheid: It's the black oot.

Duthie: There's nae a black oot the night.

Hazelheid: Oh. Dis onybody hae a shilling?

(Some jingling of change in pockets)

Duthie: I've got a washer.

Hazelheid: Perfect. We'll get it back fan the mannie empties the meter.

Duthie: Aye, except there's only washers in it.

(The lights come on)

Hazelheid: That's better. A'right, let's dee the roll call. Brother Archibald? Brother Archibald, are you here? Oh, that's right, he's haein' a fire sale the night.

Duthie: Did he get bombed?

Hazelheid: No – his fires are on sale.

Duthie: Oh, that's right. I got a rare companion set last year. It was a third aff. There wis a little shovel. And a brush. And a'thing.

Hazelheid: A'thing?

Duthie: Eh. No, jist a shovel and a brush.

Hazelheid: Nae a poker?

Duthie: No, that wis the third aff.

Hazelheid: You wis supposed ti hand in onything metal.

Duthie: Fit for?

Hazelheid: Spitfires.

Duthie: They're nae even made a' metal.

Hazelheid: How wid you ken?

Duthie: I've got een. It's made a' balsa wid. Onywye, my set wisna metal.

Hazelheid: Fit wis it?

Duthie: Bakelite.

Hazelheid: Is that fire resistant?

Duthie: No, it melted.

Hazelheid: Is Brother Benzie here?

Benzie: Oy vey iz mir!

Hazelheid: Fit like, Isaac?

Benzie: I'm nae Isaac. I'm Athol.

Hazelheid: Oh. How's Isaac?

Benzie: My dad' or my brother?

Hazelheid: Either.

Benzie: They're baith still deid.

Hazelheid: Oh, sorry. I'll mak a note a' that. The Führer'll want ti ken.

Benzie: The Führer? Hitler?

Hazelheid: No, eh, my missus. Brother Craigmyle. Are you here, Peter?

[Sound effect: Referee's whistle]

Hazelheid: Dis a'body ken oor new member, Peter Craigmyle? He's a referee.

Craigmyle: I'm nae jist 'a' referee. I'm Scotland's maist famous referee.

Benzie: So, fit dis Scotland's maist famous referee think aboot this new affside rule?

Craigmyle: Fit new affside rule?

Benzie: The een that says you hiv ti bide in your ain half. Unless you're the goalie.

Craigmyle: That'll never catch on.

Duthie: Why nae?

Craigmyle: Fa wants to see a game a fitba wi' only 28 goals? Plus yi'll need a couple a baldie boys wi' flugs runnin' up an' doon the sidelines. In fact, yi'll need sidelines. Next thing, they'll be lettin' quines play.

Hazelheid: No way. They're nae even allowed ti watch.

Craigmyle: I ken. But you mark my words. Next thing, it'll be Italians.

Hazelheid: Italians? They're a' quines ana'. Wi' their lang hair and their handbags. Naebody likes them. A'right, movin' on - Brother Codona?

Giulianotti: Brother Codona canna mak it.

Hazeleheid: Thank you, brother Giulianotti. How nae?

Giulianotti: He fell affa the Wurlitzer.

Duthie: The Waltzer?

Giulianotti: No, the Wurlitzer.

Duthie: I once fell aff the Waltzer. I went skitin' roon and roon for fifteen minutes. I nearly died.

Benzie: Fit wye fifteen minutes? The songs only lasts three minutes.

Duthie: I ken, but I pyed for five.

Hazelheid: Come on, now. Stick to the agenda! We dinna hae time for ony sidebars. A'right – Joe. Foo's yer ice-cream deein'?

Giulianotti: Brilliant, min. We've got a second flavor.

Hazelheid: Fit, vanilla?

Giulianotti: Fit's vanilla? No, Italian sassidge.

Duthie: Gads.

Giulianotti: Fit a chick. It gis great wi' the marinara.

Hazelheid: Brothers Esslemont & McIntosh?

Esslemont: Here.

Hazelheid: Did you get me a blazer yet?

Esslemont: Aye. It jist came in. It's second hand. Is that a' right?

Hazelheid: Aye. Fa's wis it?

Esslemont: Göring's.

Hazelheid: Very nice. Is it navy?

Esslemont: No, it's mair 'periwinkle'.

Duthie: I've never seen a light blue buckie.

Esslemont: It'll be perfect for your tango classes at the Locarno. Once I tak aff a' the swastikas.

Hazelheid: Well, I hope it's big enough. Brothers Hall & Russell?

Hall: Baith here.

Hazelheid: How's the shipbuilding ga'n?

Hall: It's nae. Yi ca' get steel. The bloody Jerries sunk a' the merchant ships.

Hazelheid: A'right, a'right. Nae need ti insult our Aryan brothers. Think o' them as our future trade partners.

Hall: Aye. Wait till they bomb your shipyard.

Hazelheid: Bomb? The Jerries aren'a in the business a' bombing civilian ship yards.

Hall: Only civilian hooses. Onywye, we've got a big load coming in the mor'n's mor'n.

Hazelheid: Oh, really? Brother Miller? Bruce?

Duthie: He isna coming the night.

Hazelheid: Why nae?

Duthie: He's got a punctured lung.

Hazelheid: Fae shrapnel?

Duthie: Fae bagpipes.

Hazelheid: His bagpipes exploded?

Duthie: No, the valve wis in backwards. It blew fan it should of sooked. He says ti pass on ony action items that involve musical instruments.

Hazelheid: Like fit?

Duthie: Onything but bagpipes. Or accordions.

Hazelheid: Fit wye accordions?

Duthie: They're hivvy. Fan yi'v got a punctured lung.

Hazelheid: Fit aboot a trumpet?

Duthie: That's nae hivvy. Oh. Right. Or onything you hiv ti bla'. Or sook. Or baith.

Hazelheid: Baith? Like fit?

Duthie: A moothie.

Hazelheid: Spickin' o' a sook that bla's – is Brother Wood here?

Wood: Present.

Hazelheid: Hello, John. How's the fishing ga'n?

Wood: There's nae future in it. We need ti get inti ile.

Hazelheid: North Sea?

Wood: No, Mazola.

Hazelheid: OK, brothers. Can I hae an approver for the minutes fae last month?

Wood: Wis there minutes?

Duthie: There wis nae paper.

Wood: Paperless minutes? Next it'll be paperless toilet paper.

Duthie: We already hiv paperless toilet paper. Soap.

Hazelheid: Are the minutes approved?

Wood: So approved.

Hazelheid: Seconded?

Esslemont: I'll second the minutes.

Duthie: I'll second the second. Mind and minute the seconds.

Hazelheid: OK. OK. Moving on. There's only one item on the agenda the night. I jist got a phone fae my pal, Wolfgang.

Duthie: The Nazzie?

Hazelheid: He's nae a Nazi. He's my counterpart fae the Regensburg chapter. It wis a warnin'. He said there's a Romanian Coont that's been hidin' here for the past year and a half. Apparently he's 800 years old.

Duthie: How come he's nae deid?

Hazelheid: He's a Vampire.

Duthie: Fit's a Vampire?

Hazelheid: A monster. He turns inti a bat.

Duthie: Be handy if we hid a cricket team.

Hazelheid: No. He flies aboot at night and sucks the blood a' virgins.

Duthie: We should still get him ti jine. We could use some new bleed.

Wood: Far's he ga'n ti find virgins?

Hazelheid: Exactly. That's obviously nae why he's here. He's got some ither ulterior motive. I dinna ken fit it is yet. But I'll find oot the mor'n. He invited me ti his castle, oot the road.

Wood: Dis he like fish?

Hazelheid: I dinna ken if he likes fish.

Wood: I could gie yi a fry. Nice bit a' gundy.

Duthie: Dis he hae ony spare virgins? Is ony of them quines?

Hazelheid: Shut up aboot virgins. If you ask me, though, I'll bet he's after the toon's wealth. It's an expensive business buying castles. And keeping up an army o' vampires.

Wood: Fit wealth? There's nae ony wealth in Aiberdeen. At least, nae in the fish.

Benzie: Are you kidding? Queens Road stinks a' fish. Div you ken how much is in the Common Good fund?

Wood: I thought it wis a' spent.

Benzie: That's fit Hazelheid wants you to believe. If there's nothing in the Common Good fund, naebody can moan aboot him and the cooncil squandering it. Come on, Hazelheid, tell the truth.

Hazelheid: Well, I dinna hae the exact numbers in front a' me.

Benzie: Gie's a ballpark, then.

Hazelheid: Eh, fourteen billion, twelve and six. Roon aboot.

Benzie: Fit? You wis keeping that a secret?

Hazelheid: No, I wis ga'n ti tell you. Listen. I have a dream. After the war, Aiberdeen is ga'n ti be the European City of Culture. It may not happen immediately. It may not happen until 2017. But this city will change. From dirty old granite buildings, and empty parks, and graveyards, to New World architecture and leisure spaces. Trust me – this city will be the envy of Europe. But that responsibility can't be entrusted to a bunch of elected halfwits with personal agendas.

Duthie: Fit, the cooncil?

Hazelheid: Exactly. Fae now on, Aberdeen will be run by us. The Woolmanhillati. Think about it. You lot represent eighty percent of the business money in this city. You're almost running it anyway. All we need to do is take over the Common Good Fund, and we'll be untouchable. We'll let the council take care of minor things …

Duthie: Fit kind o' minor things?

Hazelheid: I dinna ken. Pot holes. But we'll make a' the big decisions – in secret.

Benzie: Is that legal?

Hazelheid: Fa cares? My brother in law's the Chief Superintendent.

Benzie: How would you get hold of the money?

Hazelheid: My other brother in law's the manager at the Clydesdale.

Duthie: Y'er nae planning to send money ti Hitler, though, right?

Hazelheid: That's ridiculous!

Duthie: Are you nae a German?

Hazelheid: Excuse me! My family wis fae Bavaria. But I'm toonser noo.

Duthie: Are you a spy?

Hazelheid: Dinna be feel.

Duthie: My Davina thinks you're a spy

Hazelheid: How?

Duthie: 'Cause she seen you flashin' a torch aboot at Girdleness.

Hazelheid: I wis lookin' for golf ba's.

Duthie: Did you find ony?

Hazelheid: No, it wis dark. A'right then. Are we agreed? (General murmur of agreement). OK. Good. I'll tell you how my meeting went next month. AOCB? No, then I vote we adjourn.

Giulianotti: Seconded. Dis onybody funcy a cappy?

Benzie: I'll hae a 99!

Giulianotti: Fit's that?

Benzie: It's a cappy with a chocolate flake stuck in it.

Giulianotti: That'll never catch on either.

Benzie: Why nae?

Giulianotti: Chocolate wi' pepperoni? Gads.

(The meeting breaks up)

Chapter 8 - July 11, 1940. Late evening.

Slains Castle[7].
Coffin on the floor.

[Music: Vampire music]

[Sound effect: Coffin lid]

(Doricula sits up. His accent is now fully northeast).

Doricula: Ken ess? I've been in this coffin for eighteen months. Ken ess? I need a pish[8].

---

[7]Slains Castle, properly referred to as "New" Slains Castle, to differentiate it from Slains Castle (although everybody just calls it "Slains Castle"), is a ruined castle near Cruden Bay. Slains Castle is a completely different ruined castle near Collieston. By coincidence, Old Slains Castle was given to Sir Gilbert Hay (the Lord High Constable of Scotland) by his chum, King Robert I, the Bruce (aka "Spiderman One"), after Gilbert fought for him at the battles of Methven and Bannockburn and also had his pint spilled at Peep Peeps. However, many historians blame King James VI for trashing it (Slains, not Peeps) after a pub crawl in 1594. The theory that it was destroyed by a V1 Flying Bomb (aka 'Doodlebug', unrelated to James V1) has its advocates, but depends on one having flown back in time to before the inaugural launch in 1944. One local eyewitness, Doddie Hay (aged three in 1940), thinks he heard an engine cutting out, and then a bang; but that could have been his mum's Bendix spin dryer (the first, and last, in Scotland) or his dad's Humber Super Snipe crashing into a yawl. Most likely, a previous owner, John ("The Red") Comyn had it reinforced as a homer, and it just fell doon. New Slains Castle was built by Francis Hay, the 9th Earl of Erroll (or vice versa). He didn't actually build it, of course, but - according to legend - did wallpaper the scullery. The Clan Hay (aka De la Haya) featured prominently in Scottish history, politics and lemonade-making; and fought bitterly with their arch-rival Clan, Sangs. Rumour has it that Bam Stoker stayed at Slains in 1895, was bitten by a Vampire bat and immediately wrote 'Dr. Acula'. To be accurate, he didn't actually stay at Slains - it was fully booked for the Cruden Bay Flower Show and Games. Plus it was a ruin. Dr. Acula was actually inspired by Stoker's travels throughout the Carpathians; as well as by Ármin Vámbéry's 'Cluj – Far Aboot ti Bide and Bevvy', and by fellow Dubliner Sheridan Le Fanu's seminal Gothic novels: 'Carmilla', 'Spalatro' and 'Buffy Meets the Boy Fae Twilight'

[8] Courtesy of Colin Campbell, at the Aberdeen Grammar Former Pupils' Club, December 2012

[Sound effect: WW2 Air Raid Siren)]

(Wallfield tries to climb in)

Doricula: Wallfield! Fit are you deein'? Get oot o my coffin.

Wallfield: It's an air raid! I dinna want ti get bla'n up.

Doricula: You winna get bla'n up.

Wallfield: I will. I'm nae bomb-proof. I'm fragile!

Doricula: It's nae an air raid.

Wallfield: Aye it is. Can you nae hear the sireen?

Doricula: That's the doorbell.

Wallfield: Oh, right. I forgot. Fit a stupid doorbell. For a war.

Doricula: Are we expecting onybody?

Wallfield: Fit happened ti your accent?

Doricula: Nithing happened ti my accent.

Wallfield: Aye it did! Ha, ha! It's wint fae Cluj ti Clatt.

Doricula: That aye happens fan I come back.

Wallfield: Fit, every 800 years?

Doricula: You can tak the Coont oot a' Coontesswells, but you canna tak the Doric oot a' Doricula! Onywye. Fa's at the door?

Wallfield: How wid I ken?

Doricula: Are we expectin' onybody?

Wallfield: It might be the Lord Provost. I telt him you winted to spick to him. Aboot the Common Good Fund.

Doricula: That wis eighteen months ago.

Wallfield: I ken, but he nivver got back to me.

Doricula: Did you nae chase him up?

Wallfield: Aye, of course I did. I've chased him up a hale heap a' times.

Doricula: Fan?

Wallfield: Last wik. And the day.

Doricula: For Christ's sake.

Wallfield: A' right, dinna get your knickers in a twist … (he exits)

Doricula: In case you're a wondering fit's ga'n on, it's a year and half later. Thursday July the eleventh, 1940 to be exact. I wis hoping we'd hae a' the renovations finished by now, but the contractor's hopeless. I dinna think this Milne Group'll survive the war. I should've hired gypsies. Aye, the real eens fae Cluj. Nae the pretend eens fae Govan.

(Enter Wallfield with Hazelheid Van Hazelheid)

Doricula: Fa are you?

Wallfield: Wallfield.

Doricula: No, the ither boy.

Hazelheid: I'm the Lord Provost of Aiberdeen.

Wallfield: Hey, my pal Cheryl's uncle's the Provost. Is that you?

Hazelheid: Yes, that's me. Cheryl's my niece. Well, step-niece. (To Doricula). I take it you're Count Doricula. I am Abraham Van Hazelheid. But you can call me Bram.

Doricula: Bran?

Hazelheid: Bram.

Doricula: Bam?

Hazelheid: Bram. Jist ca' me 'Lord'. So, fit's up?

Doricula: I ken you're busy, so I'll be quick.

Hazelheid: Well, there is a war on.

Doricula: I ken. Fuel shortages. Bombed buildings ti bulldoze. Deid ti bury.

Hazelheid: That, and there's nae waiting for tee times.

Wallfield: Far div you play? Oh, I ken - Hazelheid. Obviously.

Hazelheid: Aye, if you want kids fae Summerhill stealing yer ba'. No, I play Balgownie.

Wallfield: I hear it's hazardous there.

Hazelheid: It is. I lost eight ba's on Friday.

Wallfield: No, I meant it's dangerous.

Hazelheid: It is. There's two unexploded Germans on the first green.

Wallfield: I wis thinkin' aboot air raids.

Hazelheid: A' the bunkers is sandbagged.

Wallfield: Far did they get a' the sand?

Hazelheid: The bunkers. Listen, though. I'm actually busy laying plans for after the war.

Wallfield: Fit, a nine holer for the wifies?

Hazelheid: Ha ha! Hardly. Well ... now you mention it. Maybe it's time we treated women as equals. Wi' the war effort and a' that. Plus it'd be nice to hae some dolly birds in the bar. No, I mean plans for the city.

Doricula: Like fit?

Hazelheid: We're ga'n ti turn St Nicholas Street and the Trinity Hall, and the Aiberdeen Market inti lovely futuristic shopping centres.

Wallfield: Div you need a solicitor?

Hazelheid: No.

Wallfield: Fit aboot a proctor?

Hazelheid: No. We're going to build communal high rise living spaces with astounding views and nae pishing allowed in the lifts. Built in our highest value real estate demographics, at Linksfield, Mastrick and Cairncry.

Wallfield: Fit aboot Seaton?

Hazelheid: Hardly. Plus, we're ga'n to build a dedicated cooncil building doon the toon. It'll be understated, and it'll blend in wi' the architecture o' Provost Skene's hoose and Marischal College. It'll bide up for hundreds a' years. The eighth wonder of the world, indeed.

Doricula: And it'll be named aifter you, nae doot.

Hazelheid: No, Sunty.

Doricula: That disna sound that visionary.

Hazelheid: Ah, but there's mair. We're going to demolish historic granite buildings in and around Union Street, and replace them with a much more aesthetically pleasing and mould- and rust-resistant miracle. Concrete. We're not going to let Aberdeen suffer the same urban blight as its European neighbors. We're not going to make the same mistakes as Rome, Madrid and Paris. We're going to repurpose theatres and cinemas and churches – places that naebody gis - as bingo halls, and then as pubs. Banks as coffee shops. We'll force historic family businesses to close down and be replaced by mobile phone shops and fast food joints. And eventually we're ga'n ti fill in Union Terrace Gairdens with cement and turn it inti a car park.

Doricula: That's horrible.

Hazelheid: I ken – but it's fit the minkers want! But fit div you want to see me aboot?

Wallfield: Can I tell him?

Hazelheid: Fa are you onywye?

Wallfield: I telt yi. Wallfield. The boy that phoned you. I'm in charge o' the Coont's legal and real estate matters.

Hazelheid: You're joking.

Wallfield: I'm nae joking. I'm a trained solicitor.

Hazelheid: A solicitor? What's your specialty?

Wallfield: Benny Yorston - 1927 to 1931. No, I mean selling castles.

Doricula: It's aboot my Common Good Fund.

Hazelheid: 'Your' Common Good Fund? The Common Good Fund is for the Common Good of the folk a' Aiberdeen. That's why it's ca'd the 'Common Good Fund'.

Doricula: Aye. That's fit yi'd like people ti think. It's actually to pay for your Daimler, and send your coonciller chums on fact-finding jaunts ti' twin cities. I'm sure you've pocketed a few quid ana'.

Hazelheid: That's slander, that.

Doricula: Wallfield - read him the Bill of Sale.

Wallfield: (opens Bill of Sale, a scroll). "February 12 1920. Know all men by these presents that I Abraham Van Hazelheid, of Rubislaw Den South, Aberdeen, for & in Consideration of the Sum of Two million pounds, twelve shillings & six pence sterling payed by Aberdeen City Council on behalf of the Common Good Fund do bargain sell & deliver unto the said Council the lands comprising the estate of Hazelheid".

Hazelheid: Far did you get that?

Doricula: Never mind far I got it. That two million quid came oot o' my account at the Clydesdale.

Wallfield: Two million twelve and six.

Doricula: Which means, either the council owes me two million quid, or it owes me Hazelheid.

Hazelheid: The council disna hae that much money.

Wallfield: Rubbish. Fit aboot a' that visionary rubbish? Far's a' that money coming fae?

Hazelheid: Neen o' your business! We need that money. To rebuild the city after the war. The minkers – sorry, the voters – sorry, the people - don't want a historic Granite City. They're nae interested in listed buildings. They dinna want a doon toon. They want a brand new City. They want suburbs. Cooncil hooses. A motor car for every two hooses! Bingo. Bars. Flumes! Gie you two million? O'er my deid body!

(Hazelheid exits)

Wallfield: I think that went well. Luckily we didna mention The Forest a' Stocket. (Hazelheid's head pops back in)

Hazelheid: I heard that. You're nae getting the Forest a' Stocket either. (Hazelheid's head pops back out).

Doricula: Aye, well done. I was ga'n ti save that for Christmas.

(Doricula begins to leave).

Wallfield: Far you gan?

Doricula: For a pint.

Wallfield: Lager?

Doricula: Bleed.

Wallfield: Fa's?

Doricula: Cheryl's.

Wallfield: You leave her alone!

Doricula: It's neen of your business.

Wallfield: Aye it is. Clint's my pal. Get your ain bit a' stuff.

Doricula: I'm nae interested in bits a' stuff.

Wallfield: Oh, sorry. Are you, you ken … ? (nods).

Doricula: No, it's nae that. I used ti be a bit o' a lad mysel'.

Wallfield: Wis you ever mairied?

Doricula: Aye. Forty three times.

Wallfield: Kids?

Doricula: Twenty eight million.

Wallfield: How div you tell them apart?

Doricula: I dinna. They're a' bats.

Wallfield: Div you keep in touch wi' your exes?

Doricula: Jist fan I dig them up.

Wallfield: So, you're nae dating right now?

Doricula: No, I gid a' that up.

Wallfield: Fit wye?

Doricula: Well, aifter aboot six hundred years, you realize. A' the good looking eens is mental. And the eens that arena' mental are feel.

Wallfield: So, did you hae sex wi' Cheryl?

Doricula: No. I just drunk her bleed.

Wallfield: She said she cut hersel' shaving.

Doricula: She did. I jist sooked the cloot. Fit are you worried aboot onywye? Div you funcy her?

Wallfield: I've aye funcied her.

Doricula: Since fan?

Wallfield: Since the day I seen her bunions.

Doricula: Fan was that?

Wallfield: That night at the castle.

Doricula: I seen mair than her bunions.

Wallfield: So did I. But she's got rare bunions.

Doricula: Well, tough luck. I'm drinking Cheryl's bleed the night and there's nithin' you can dee aboot it!

Wallfield: Aye, o'er my deid body!

Doricula: You ana'? Nae problem (he leans over and bites Wallfield's neck).

Wallfield: Ow! That wis sair. Oh, I dinna feel right. I think I'm ga'n to fint … (he slides to the floor)

Doricula: That'll keep him quiet for a few hoors. (Exits)

(Wallfield regains consciousness; remains on the floor).

Wallfield: Far am I? Fit's my name? Oh, aye, I mind now. I better warn Hazelheid. Far's the phone? Oh, here it is on the fleer – that's right handy. (Dials)

(Sound effect: Rotary phone dialing)

Wallfield: Of course, he winna be there yet. Telt yi – voicemail. Oh, hello. Mr. Bam? It's me, Wallfield, again. Listen, I need to warn you. My boss. Coont Doricula? Div you mind him? Well, he's a Vampire, and he's in love wi' Cheryl. In fact, he's awa' to drink Cheryl's bleed the night. Thank you. Have a nice day. Oh, by the way, could you send an ambliance? Oh, no nivver mind, I'll dee that.

(Wallfield passes out again)

Chapter 9 - July 12, 1940, Morning.

An office at Aberdeen City Cooncil
Abraham Van Hazelheid is at his desk.
Kingseat knocks at the door.
(Enter Kingseat)

Hazelheid: Ah, Dr. Kingseat. Thank you for coming so quickly.

Kingseat: No need for formality. Just call me 'Doctor'. Now, what seems to be the problem?

Hazelheid: It's nae me. Have you heard of Coont Doricula?

Kingseat: Of course. The Vampire. What's wrong with him?

Hazelheid: Nothing. He's here.

Kingseat: (looks around - panicky) Here?

Hazelheid: No, nae here.

Kingseat: You said here.

Hazelheid: I meant here in Aiberdeen.

Kingseat: Where in Aiberdeen?

Hazelheid: Cruden Bay.

Kingseat: That's nae in Aiberdeen.

Hazelheid: It's close.

Kingseat: No it's nae. It's 23.3 miles.

Hazelheid: Close, as opposed to Cluj.

Kingseat: Ah. The ancestral home of Doricula. 1,890 miles fae the Castlegate.

Hazelheid: Aye, if you ging through France. It's only 1,853 if you ging through Belgium.

Kingseat: I ken. But there's aye a hud up at the roondaboot in Liege.

Hazelheid: Nae now.

Kingseat: Did they pit in the new bypass?

Hazelheid: No, the Jerries blew it up. But the cooncil's ga'n ti build anither een.

Kingseat: Fan?

Hazelheid: 2017.

Kingseat: Oh, that is quick for a cooncil! Far wid they get money for that?

Hazelheid: Brussels.

Kingseat: Is there that much money in sprouts?

Hazelheid: No, waffles. We've applied for money ana'.

Kingseat: Fit for?

Hazelheid: A hale heap a things. A zoo at Hazelheid. A Winter Gardens at the Duthie Park. A conservatory.

Kingseat: Far aboot?

Hazelheid: My hoose. Plus, a Ring Road.

Kingseat: Fit's a Ring Road?

Hazelheid: A bypass.

Kingseat: Fit, a circular route a' aroon' Aiberdeen?

Hazelheid: No. A straight line, fae Garthdee ti Great Northern Road.

Kingseat: Fit for?

Hazelheid: Ti link the airport to the ski slope.

Kingseat: Fit for?

Hazelheid: The Winter Olympics.

Kingseat: Fit Winter Olympics?

Hazelheid: 2018.

Kingseat: That's in Korea.

Hazelheid: Aye, right. Fan dis it sna in Korea?

Kingseat: Fit aboot the Ryder Cup in 2018?

Hazelheid: We're haein' that ana'.

Kingseat: Far?

Hazelheid: Either the nine-holer at Hazelheid, or Auchmill.

Kingseat: Fit aboot Balgownie?

Hazelheid: You hiv ti be a member.

Kingseat: So, far aboot's this ski slope?

Hazelheid: We're building the world's biggest practice slope, at Garthdee.

Kingseat: Oot a fit? Sna?

Hazelheid: Recycled materials.

Kingseat: Spitfires?

Hazelheid: Rubber doormats. Onywye, I wid ging through Belgium.

Kingseat: I widna.

Hazelheid: How nae?

Kingseat: You hiv ti ging right through Dunkirk.

Hazelheid: And?

Kingseat: It's a' full a' Jerries.

Hazelheid: Aye, peace-keeping troops.

Kingseat: Nae peace-keeping. The Zed Zed.

Hazelheid: Ess Ess.

Kingseat: Aye. They're shootin' a'body.

Hazelheid: Jist the Resistance.

Kingseat: Nae jist the Resistance. City Cooncillors.

Hazelheid: No way. Fit wye wid they shoot cooncillors?

Kingseat: Karma. But nae jist cooncillors. Women, kids, al' folk. Jews, poofs, gypsies, imbeciles.

Hazelheid: Can yi' say 'poofs'?

Kingseat: Aye. It's 1940.

Hazelheid: Fa wid shoot gypsies?

Kingseat: Fa widna? No, I'm kidding. They paved my driveway last wik. Fit a rare job. Cheap. Mind you, my neighbor wisna happy.

Hazelheid: Wis he jealous?

Kingseat: No. They used his pavin' steens. Onywye, they've shot thoosands a Belgians. And Frogs.

Hazelheid: The gypsies?

Kingseat: No, the Nazzies.

Hazelheid: Aye, right. Name one person that got shot.

Kingseat: My uncle Bing.

Hazelheid: Bing Kingseat?

Kingseat: Aye.

Hazelheid: Dis he sing?

Kingseat: No, he's deid.

Hazelheid: Wis it a firing squad?

Kingseat: No, he drooned. He wis on the Lusitania.

Hazelheid: Oh, that wis tragic. It went doon in seconds.

Kingseat: Aye, he wisna on it fan it sunk.

Hazelheid: Far did he droon?

Kingseat: The Uptown Baths.

Hazelheid: Could he nae swim?

Kingseat: Of course he could. He did a belly flop aff the top board.

Hazelheid: I've done a belly flop aff the top board.

Kingseat: Aye, but he missed the watter.

Hazelheid: So how did he droon?

Kingseat: In the shower.

Hazelheid: You said he got shot.

Kingseat: Aye, he did.

Hazelheid: Far? Dunkirk?

Kingseat: No, Codona's. He's still got the BB in his nose.

Hazelheid: I thought he wis deid.

Kingseat: He is, but he's still got the BB in his nose. Onywye, back ti Cruden Bay. Far's this boy Doricula bidin'?

Hazelheid: Slains Castle.

Kingseat: So, fit div you need me for?

Hazelheid: You're the only Vampire slayer in Aiberdeen.

Kingseat: No, I'm nae.

Hazelheid: There's mair?

Kingseat: No, I'm jist nae een. I thought _you_ wis a Vampire Slayer.

Hazelheid: I'm nae a Vampire slayer. Jist a hunter.

Kingseat: You dinna kill them?

Hazelheid: No. I'm a non-violent person. Plus I fint at the sight a' bleed.

Hazelheid: How come you're listed under 'Vampire Slayers' in the Evening Express?

Kingseat: It's anither three guineas to get listed under 'Doctors'.

Hazelheid: Have you excised any hearts?

Kingseat: Beating?

Hazelheid: Aye.

Kingseat: No.

Hazelheid: But you've excised nae-beating hearts?

Kingseat: No.

Hazelheid: So fit hiv yi excised?

Kingseat: Polyps.

Hazelheid: Have you done ony decapitations?

Kingseat: No. I once cut aff a lug by mistake.

Hazelheid: As opposed to deliberately? That's close enough. Tell me. What you do know about me?

Kingseat: Em … let me see. Abraham Van Hazelheid, better known as 'Bam'. German spy.

Hazelheid: It's nae 'Bam'? It's 'Bram'. And I'm nae a German Spy.

Kingseat: A Russian spy?

Hazelheid: I'm nae a spy.

Kingseat: A'body thinks you are.

Hazelheid: Fit are you spickin' aboot?

Kingseat: Div you deny that you're the high heidyin o' the Aiberdeen Illuminatis?

Hazelheid: Rubbish! Far did you hear that?

Kingseat: It wis in The Leopard. Right after a riveting article aboot riveting; and afore two excellent exposés, one aboot Snuffy Ivy[9], and one aboot pra'n pluffers lung.

Hazelheid: OK, it's true. I am the High Grand Master of the Aiberdeen Order of the Illuminati.

Kingseat: The Woolmanhillati?

Hazelheid: Yes.

Kingseat: So it DIS exist. Can I jine?

Hazelheid: We dinna tak jist onybody

Kingseat: How come you got in? Wis you a fag at Gordonstoun?

Hazelheid: I wisna a fag at Gordonstoun.

Kingseat: Far wis you a fag at?

Hazelheid: Naewye. Fit wye Gordonstoun?

Kingseat: The German School.

Hazelheid: It's nae German.

Kingseat: Aye it is. I kint a German boy that gid there.

Hazelheid: Fa?

Kingseat: I canna mind his hale name. Philip something something.

---

[9] http://mcjazz.f2s.com/Prostitution.htm

Hazelheid: Philip Schleswig-Holstein-Sonderburg-Glücksburg?

Kingseat: Aye. Prince Philip.

Hazelheid: He's nae a German. He's Greek.

Kingseat: That lot's a' Germans. Div you ken him?

Hazelheid: Nae really. I ken he's chummy wi' King Dod's dother.

Hazelheid: Ken Dodd?

Kingseat: No, King Dod.

Hazelheid: Is she nae jist fourteen?

Kingseat: Aye, but they hiv a chaperone. Well, they did fan I seen them.

Hazelheid: Far aboot?

Kingseat: The flecky Belmont. You kent Gordonstoun wis founded by anither German spy?

Hazelheid: Fit, Kurt Hahn? He's nae German.

Kingseat: Fit is he?

Hazelheid: Jewish. He got kicked oot a' Germany.

Kingseat: Fit for?

Hazelheid: He ca'd Hitler a feel gype.

Kingseat: So how did you get inti the Illuminati?

Hazelheid: I wis born into it.

Kingseat: Far aboot?

Hazelheid: Bavaria. I'm the great great great great great great grandson of Adam Weishaupt. I tell a lie. Jist five greats.

Kingseat: Wis he the founder of the Bavarian Illuminati?

Hazelheid: Aye.

Kingseat: Fan did you leave Bavaria?

Hazelheid: My family buggered aff in 1864. Fan Bismarck took o'er Prussia.

Kingseat: So, how come you're ca'd "Hazelheid"?

Hazelheid: It wis that or "White Heid".

Kingseat: So what do you know about me?

Hazelheid: I ken you wis a gynaecologist.

Kingseat: Nae a gynaecologist. A proctologist.

Hazelheid: Far did you learn proctology?

Kingseat: Gordonstoun.

Hazelheid: Div they teach proctology at Gordonstoun?

Kingseat: No, I jist picked it up.

Hazelheid: I heard you wis struck aff.

Kingseat: I wisna struck aff. I teen early retirement.

Hazelheid: Fit for?

Kingseat: Ti spend mair time wi' my family.

Hazelheid: Aye, right. Fit happened?

Kingseat: I think it was that time I hid sex wi' a patient. It wis a' blown oot a' proportion.

Hazelheid: Did she consent?

Kingseat: He.

Hazelheid: Did he consent?

Kingseat: Aye, to the anesthetic.

Hazelheid: War dis strange things to men.

Kingseat: It wis twenty years ago.

Hazelheid: Never mind a' that. I need you to help me kill Doricula.

Kingseat: It's impossible.

Hazelheid: Why? Oh – the Hippocratic Oath?

Kingseat: No, I never took the oath. I slept in that day.

Hazelheid: Night shift?

Kingseat: Fourteen pints.

Hazelheid: Why impossible, then?

Kingseat: He's indestructible.

Hazelheid: No, he his a weak spot.

Kingseat: Fit?

Hazelheid: Apparently he's in love with my niece. Cheryl Noble.

Kingseat: I didna ken she wis your niece.

Hazelheid: Well, step-niece. Div you ken her?

Kingseat: Nae really. Her mum was a patient a' mine. Fan she wis alive.

Hazelheid: Oh, nae now she's deid?

Kingseat: No. How dis Doricula ken your niece?

Hazelheid: She bade wi' Doricula on her holidays. The Hogmanay afore last.

Kingseat: Cruden Bay?

Hazelheid: Cluj. It wis an engagement present.

Kingseat: She got engaged to a Vampire?

Hazelheid: Clint's nae a Vampire.

Kingseat: Fa's Clint?

Hazelheid: Her boyfriend.

Kingseat: She's got a boyfriend and a fiuncé?

Hazelheid: No, she disna hae a fiuncé. They never got engaged. They broke it aff. But they're getting engaged again, the mor'n.

Kingseat: Dis he ken he's in love with her?

Hazelheid: I suppose. He proposed ti' her.

Kingseat: No, I mean, dis Clint ken Doricula loves her?

Hazelheid: Clint's a him.

Kingseat: No, dis Clint ken Doricula loves Cheryl?

Hazelheid: I dinna ken. Onywye, that's why we're ga'n ti kill him.

Kingseat: Clint?

Hazelheid: Doricula.

Kingseat: How come you ken Doricula's in love wi' her?

Hazelheid: I got a voicemail fae this boy Wallfield.

Kingseat: Fa's he?

Hazelheid: The boy that won them the engagement present. He used ti work wi' Clint.

Kingseat: Fit dis he dee now?

Hazelheid: He works for Doricula.

Kingseat: Dis he funcy Cheryl?

Hazelheid: I dinna ken. But he said Doricula wis ga'n ti see her last night.

Kingseat: Fit for?

Hazelheid: Fit div you think?

Kingseat: A shag.

Hazelheid: Oh. I nivver thought o' that.

Kingseat: Good luck ti him.

Hazelheid: How?

Kingseat: Vampires only ging for virgins.

Hazelheid: She's hopin' ti be a virgin soon. Onywye, I'm nae takkin' the chunce. You ken fit they say aboot bleed.

Kingseat: It brings you oot in blisters?

Hazelheid: No, it's thicker than watter.

Kingseat: Of course it is. It is watter – wi' bleed cells. It's like black pudding soup.

Hazelheid: No, nae literally. It's a proverb. Like 'People who live in glass houses shouldn't throw stones'.

Kingseat: Aye, that's true. Especially indoors. Oh, I get it. It's nae literally aboot steens.

Hazelheid: That's right.

Kingseat: It could be a frying pan. Or dazzies. I'll tell you though, I'm nae buying it.

Hazelheid: Nae buying fit?

Kingseat: You deein' something for family. I ken your reputation. Guaranteed you hiv some ither interest.

Hazelheid: Interest in fit?

Kingseat: In killing the Vampire.

Hazelheid: Fit possible interest could I hae?

Kingseat: I dinna ken. Money, influence, power, fame. Sex.

Hazelheid: Rubbish. There's nae fame involved.

Kingseat: Aye right. We'll see. So what's the plan?

Hazelheid: We go oe'r ti the castle afore it's dark, I'll open his coffin, you pit a stake through his heart, cut it oot and set it on fire.

Kingseat: Fit, the stake?

Hazelheid: No, his heart.

Kingseat: Hearts dinna catch light.

Hazelheid: Well, bring lighter fluid.

Kingseat: I dinna smoke.

Hazelheid: Paraffin, then.

Kingseat: I hiv a coal fire.

Hazelheid: Yi canna tak a coal fire.

Kingseat: I'm nae. I'm jist sayin' I dinna hae paraffin.

Hazelheid: I wish I hid a coal fire. I ging through three gallon a paraffin a day.

Kingseat: In July?

Hazelheid: It gets nippy.

Kingseat: Tak your paraffin, then.

Hazelheid: It's a' deen. You must hae something flammable on you.

Kingseat: Sherry.

Hazelheid: That'll dee. OK. Then we'll cut his heid aff wi' an axe and bury it at a crossroads.

Kingseat: The axe?

Hazelheid: No, his heid. Is that clear?

Kingseat: Aye. No. One question. Fit's in it for me?

Hazelheid: Same as me. You'll be saving Clint & Cheryl's marriage.

Kingseat: Forget it.

Hazelheid: How about twenty guineas? And the axe.

Kingseat: Done. OK, let's go

Hazelheid: Aye we will. Nae right now, though. I hiv to open the new Ice Rink this aifterneen. D'you funcy ga'n?

Kingseat: I'll pass. I hate ice. Ever since I wis on the Titanic.

Hazelheid: You wis on the Titanic?

Kingseat: Aye. I wis the Medical Officer. It wis a disaster.

Hazelheid: I ken. It sunk.

Kingseat: No, that's fan I cut the lug aff.

Hazelheid: Oh, fan it hit the iceberg?

Kingseat: No, fan I wis bleezing. But there wis good news and good news.

Hazelheid: Fit wis the good news?

Kingseat: The lug wisna malignant.

Hazelheid: Fit wis the ither good news?

Kingseat: The boy drooned.

Hazelheid: So, fit wis the real story? I mean, how could the Captain be that negligent to hit an iceberg?

Kingseat: It wisna the Captain. It wis some pair a' feels in a canoe. They hid ti swerve ti miss them. It wis a loon and his bit a' fluff. Fae Aiberdeen, apparently.

Hazelheid: Fa wis it? Somebody fae the AU Rowing Club, obviously.

Kingseat: I've nae idea. I wis busy sewing on a lug. Onywye, I'll never ging back on the ice.

Hazelheid: Oh come on, it'll be a laugh. Fit's the worst that could happen? It's nae as if one of oor bombers is ga'n ti crash inti it, or onything - right?

Kingseat: "Oor" bombers?

Hazelheid: Aye. RAF of course.

Kingseat: Fit wid RAF bombers be deein' up here?

Hazelheid: Did I say bombers? I meant … eh, fighters. No, practice bombing. Eh …

Kingseat: OK, the ice rink it is. But I'm nae ga'n on it.

Hazelheid: But first, your nephew Clint's office.

Kingseat: Are you buyin' a hoose?

Hazelheid: No, I'm nae buyin' a hoose. I've got a hoose.

Kingseat: So far exactly dis the Provost bide? Provost Skene's Hoose? No wait, Provost Watt Drive?

Hazelheid: No, I dinna tell onybody far I bide. That information could fa inti the enemy's hands. But I will tell you, it's the only cooncil hoose in Rubislaw Den.

Kingseat: Why are we ga'n ti see Clint?

Hazelheid: I need ti find oot if your loon'll help us kill the Vampire.

Kingseat: Fit for?

Hazelheid: Somebody his to keep Wallfield oot o' the wye.

Kingseat: Div you think Wallfield wid interfere? Did he nae jist warn you?

Hazelheid: Aye, but you never ken. Fan the Vampire's in the room, onything can happen. He can hypnotize you wi' jist a look.

Kingseat: I never kint that. Coont me oot.

Hazelheid: I though you wis a Vampire expert.

Kingseat: I never said I wis an expert. I jist said I wis listed as een. It's my back-up specialist subject.

Hazelheid: For fit?

Kingseat: Disastermind.

Hazelheid: Fit's your first subject? Proctology?

Kingseat: Lugs.

Hazelheid: Come on, let's go. Div you hae a car?

Kingseat: No. Can we nae jist ging in your Provost car?

Hazelheid: No, it's oot a' paraffin. We'll get the bus.

Kingseat: Fae Broad Street to Chapel Street? We could jist walk.

Hazelheid: Fit, and get machine gunned wi' a Stuka?

Kingseat: A Stuka? Stukas canna fly as far as Aiberdeen.

Hazelheid: Aye they can. Wi' their new fuel tanks. In fact they're coming the day. Fae Stavanger.

Kingseat: How wid you ken a that?

Hazelheid: Eh, intelligence.

Kingseat: Intelligence? Aiberdeen? Should you nae tell a'body?

Hazelheid: I will, at the ice rink. Come on, we'll miss the bus.

Kingseat: Hiv you got bussies?

Hazelheid: No. It's OK, we'll swick on. I aye div.

(They exit)

Chapter 10 - July 12, 1940, Afternoon.

Aiberdein Considine.
Clint is at his desk.
(Enter Van Hazelheid and Kingseat)

Clint: Hullo?

Hazelheid: Are you Clint Eastneuk?

Clint: Aye. Fa are you?

Kingseat: I'm Dr. Kingseat.

Clint: I ken you.

Kingseat: How div yi ken me?

Clint: I seen you at my hoose fan I wis little. My ma said you wis a gynaecologist.

Kingseat: Procotologist.

Clint: Oh. Like Wallfield?

Kingseat: He's a proctor.

Clint: (gesturing toward Hazelheid) So, fa's he?

Hazelheid: I'm Abraham Van Hazelheid.

Clint: Fit, Bam? Cheryl's uncle?

Hazelheid: Bram. Step uncle.

Clint: I ken your wife. She cleans oor hoose.

Kingseat: I didna ken you wis mairied.

Hazelheid: I'm nae. She went aff wi' a buccaneer.

Kingseat: A buccaneer fae far?

Hazelheid: Buchan.

Kingseat: Fit's her name?

Hazelheid: Hazel.

Kingseat: Hazel Hazelheid?

Hazelheid: Aye. It used ti be.

Kingseat: Fit is it now?

Hazelheid: Hazel Pugwash.

Kingseat: Fit's her maiden name?

Hazelheid: Bank-Dairy.

Kingseat: You hid yer wife oot cleanin' hooses? Is that fit wye she left?

Hazelheid: Well, Provosts mak a pittance.

Kingseat: Fit aboot buccaneers?

Hazelheid: Oh, it's hand ti mooth, bein' a pirate nowadays.

Kingseat: Fit wye? Nae treasure?

Hazelheid: U-boats. And unions.

Kingseat: Fit union is the pirates?

Hazelheid: The pirates union.

Kingseat: Oh. You could've got anither job.

Hazelheid: I hinna time. I'm busy. Plannin' a' the rebuildin'.

Kingseat: Fit rebuilding?

Hazelheid: Fae a' the bombs that's coming the day.

Kingseat: Bombs the day? How div you ken aboot bombs? You are a spy.

Hazelheid: I'm nae a spy! I jist keep my lugs ti' the grun'. I am the Lord Provost. And the heid o' the Woolmanhillati.

Clint: I thought that wis secret.

Hazelheid: Oh, aye. I forgot.Kingseat: Clint – we need to ask you about Cheryl.

Clint: Is she a'right?

Kingseat: Fan did you see her last?

Clint: This morning. We jist got engaged.

Kingseat: Aye, Bam telt me.

Hazelheid: Bram.

Kingseat: Hiv you seen her since?

Clint: No, I'm seein' her the morn'. We're supposed ti be getting' anither ring.

Hazelheid: I could sell you a real diamond ring. Cheap.

Clint: Nah, I widna want to impose.

Hazelheid: It widna be imposing. It's your mum's ring.

Clint: How come yiv got my mum's ring?

Hazelheid: She gid it back ti me. She broke aff oor engagement.

Clint: You wis engaged ti my ma? Before my da?

Hazelheid: I am your da.

Clint: You're nae my da. My da's Jimmy Eastneuk. He works for the Co-opy. And he's a war hero.

Kingseat: Fit kind a' hero?

Clint: He chored a German machine gun.

Kingseat: Fae a machine gun nest?

Clint: No, fae Cocky Hunters.

Hazelheid: Far is he now?

Clint: He's back in Frunce. Wi' my mum.

Kingseat: Wi' Bunty? Fit are they deein' in Frunce?

Clint: They're on their holidays.

Hazelheid: Div they ken the Germans invaded Frunce last wik?

Clint: Aye, but the Co-opy only gis them the Trades' fortnight.

Hazelheid: How did they get there?

Clint: Cycled.

Kingseat: How did they get across the Channel?

Clint: Stabilizers. So how come you think you're my da?

Hazelheid: I hid relations wi Bunty.

Kingseat: Fan?

Hazelheid: 1885. 1886, 7, 8 and 9. And 1920.

Clint: I wis born in 1886.

Kingseat: Aye. March 15th.

Hazelheid: How div you ken?

Kingseat: I delivered you. Fan you wis a baby.

Hazelheid: I thought you wis a proctologist.

Kingseat: It wis a difficult birth.

Hazelheid: I aye thought it wis a coincidence that Clint's mum and Cheryl's mum were baith ca'd Bunty.

Kingseat: It's nae a coincidence. They're twins.

Hazelheid: I didna ken that. I hid sex wi' the ither Bunty ana'.

Kingseat: Me too.

Clint: Fit!? You hid sex wi' Cheryl's mum?

Kingseat: I hid sex wi' baith Bunties. Aye, nae at the same time. Well, jist the once.

Clint: I never kint the ither Bunty. She died fan I wis little. They say you couldna tell them apart.

Kingseat: I could tell them apart. I am an astute diagnostician. Your mum his a little mole on the left buttock. Or is it the right? And Cheryl's mum wis a dwarf.

Clint: Dis that mean Cheryl's my sister?

Kingseat: Only if I'm actually your da, and hers. Or he is. Or somebody else is.

Clint: So I could be her brither. Fit's the chunces?

Kingseat: Speaking as a medical professional, I've nae idea. But I'm guessing it's aboot one in five, or more. Or less.

Hazelheid: It's lucky you two never hid sex

Clint: Aye that's affa lucky. (coughs) That dis it. The engagement's aff.

Hazelheid: So, will you help us kill the Vampire?

Clint: Fit's the Vampire got ti dee wi' it?

Hazelheid: He wis wi' Cheryl last night. And he'll be wi' her the night ana'. Will you help us kill him?

Clint: No way. She brought this on hersel'. She led him on in Cluj. I'm nae killin' naebody.

Hazelheid: Ah, right, never mind. We'll dee it oorsels. So you dinna want the ring?

Clint: Ask the proctologist fit di tee wi' the ring.

Hazelheid: A'right. You made yer point. Come on, Kingseat, let's go open that Ice Rink.

Clint: Hey, I'm meetin' my pals at the Ice Rink. I'll see you there.

Hazelheid: Nae if we see you first!

Kingseat: (aside To Hazelheid, out of Clint's hearing). Come here.

Hazelheid: Fit?

Kingseat: Shhh! Div we hiv ti attend this ice rink do?

Hazelheid: Aye. I hiv ti cut the ribbon. An dee a figure a' one.

Kingseat: You mean a figure a' eight.

Hazelheid: No - a one. I canna dee an eight. I canna even dee a curve.

Kingseat: Well dinna fa' doon.

Hazelheid: I aye fa' doon.

Kingseat: I ken. It's hard to bide up on skates. On icebergs.

Hazelheid: Skates? I'm spicking aboot wellies. I thought you nivver wint on ice.

Kingseat: I dinna. But I love curling. Aye, spectating. Onywye, I hope we dinna hiv ti bide. Ice rinks is aye freezing. For some reason.

Hazelheid: Div yi nae get cal' watching curling?

Kingseat: No, I dinna ging in person.

Hazelheid: Oh – you hiv a TV.

Kingseat: No. Jist a radio.

Hazelheid: Well, there's nae rush. We dinna want to be in Cruden Bay till jist afore sun-up. If we start cycling aboot four pm we'll be OK.

Kingseat: Cycling? Can we nae get the bus?

Hazelheid: There's nae a bus.

Kingseat: Nae even a BlueBird?

Hazelheid: No. Only services essential ti the war effort.

Kingseat: Like fit?

Hazelheid: The Tour a' City & Suburbs.

Kingseat: Dis that ging ti Cruden Bay?

Hazelheid: No, it gings ti my hoose.

Kingseat: How's that essential?

Hazelheid: How else wid the cooncillors get oot for my "Chemin-de-Fer and Shortbreed" nights? Hey, fit are you deein' wi' that bicycle pump? Dinna you touch my ring! Ow!!!

Chapter 11 - July 13 1940, Just before dawn.

The basement of Slains Castle

[Music: Vampire music]

(Enter Kingseat and Hazelheid. Hazelheid is wearing wellies)

Kingseat: I'm knackered!

Hazelheid: Shut up. Yiv done nithing but moan the hale wye oot.

Kingseat: You never said it wis a tandem.

Hazelheid: So?

Kingseat: You never pedalled once.

Hazelheid: Aye I did.

Kingseat: No you didna.

Hazelheid: How wid you ken? You wis at the front.

Kingseat: There's nae pedals at the back.

Hazelheid: I wis skitin' my wellies on the grun.

Kingseat: Aye – like a brake. That wisna the worst. A'thing wis missin'.

Hazelheid: There's a war on. Fit did you expect? A bell?

Kingseat: Handlebars. A saddle.

Hazelheid: At least there wis tyres.

Kingseat: You hid a tyre. I winna be able to sit on the cludgie for a wik.

Hazelheid: Spickin' a fit, is oor freen' fae Cluj back?

Kingseat: Let me check. (Opens the coffin)

[Sound effect: Coffin lid]

Kingseat: No – the coffin's empty.
[Sound effect: Coffin lid]

Hazelheid: Good. It'll be light in aboot ten minutes. We better get ready for him. Did you bring the stake?

Kingseat: Fit stake? I thought you wis bringing the stake.

Hazelheid: Fit aboot the axe?

Kingseat: Far wis I ga'n ti get an axe?

Hazelheid: Well, fit hiv you got for cutting oot hearts and cuttin' aff heids?

Kingseat: I've got a thoracotomy kit and a saw.

Hazelheid: That's perfect!

Kingseat: Aye, at hame. I've got a nail file and a pencil.

Hazelheid: H?

Kingseat: B.

Hazelheid: Dammit. We'll jist hae ti improvise. A' right, let's get ready for the confession.

Kingseat: Fit confession?

Hazelheid: We need ti prepare – spiritually.

Kingseat: Spiritually? Actually I could dee wi' a nip.

Hazelheid: No. Listen. Doricula is cunning, right?

Kingseat: Aye ...

Hazelheid: He's ga'n to try to every trick in the Vampire book.

Kingseat: Fit Vampire book?

Hazelheid: Nae an actual book. He's ga'n ti play us against each ither. He's ga'n ti try ti exploit our slightest weakness.

Kingseat: So you mean ...?

Hazelheid: Aye. We hiv ti confess oor maist intimate secrets.

Kingseat: So, onything he says ...

Hazelheid: We should ken already - or, ken ti be a lie!

Kingseat: I hivna got ony secrets.

Hazelheid: Aye, right. Start aff little.

Kingseat: Like fit?

Hazelheid: Like, I've sput on a bus.

Kingseat: OK. I've sput on a bus.

Hazelheid: Upstairs?

Kingseat: No, fae the bus stop.

Hazelheid: Did you hit it?

Kingseat: No, I hit the wifie behind me. It wis windy. Fit aboot you?

Hazelheid: Same. But I hit my glaises. Then I hit the bus.

Kingseat: Wi' your second attempt?

Hazelheid: No, wi' my bike.

Kingseat: Oh, fae nae eyesight?

Hazelheid: No, fae nae brakes.

Kingseat: Wis it a Raleigh?

Hazelheid: No, it wis jist me. Your turn.

Kingseat: A'right. I pick my nose.

Hazelheid: A'body picks their nose.

Kingseat: Wi' a fork?

Hazelheid: I peed aff the top o' the Toon's Hoose.

Kingseat: A'body's done that.

Hazelheid: Aye, but I wis trying ti hit my chauffeur.

Kingseat: I gob in folk's pints fan they're nae lookin'.

Hazelheid: I gob in folk's pints fan they are lookin'.

Kingseat: I shite in a bag on folks' doorsteps, set fire ti it, and ring the doorbell.

Hazelheid: I shite on folks' doorsteps and spoon it through the letterbox.

Kingseat: I fart in the bath and collect the bubbles in a cup.

Hazelheid: I canna beat that!

Kingseat: I can – I pit my dad inti Kingseat and he killed himsel'.

Hazelheid: Kingseat pit Kingseat into Kingseat? Wis he mad?

Kingseat: Well, he wisna affa happy aboot it ...

Hazelheid: Look! The sun's coming up!

[Sound effect: Big Door Creaking]

Hazelheid: He's coming back! Wi' Cheryl! Quick, hide behind that pillar! (They hide)

(Enter Doricula & Cheryl. Unseen by anyone, Wallfield creeps in behind them & also hides, behind a different pillar)

Cheryl: (Not happy) You can pit me doon, thank you.

Doricula: I thought you liked flyin'.

Cheryl: Aye, inside a balloon. Nae hingin' fae een.

Doricula: You said you fancied a toor.

100

Cheryl: Aye, nae the Wallace Toor. And nae up the erse. You must be blind.

Doricula: Aye. As a bat. I dinna see at night. I ging by high-pitched sounds. But nae right in my lug.

Cheryl: Well, I'm sorry. I aye scream fan I fa' in the harbour.

Doricula: You said you funcied a dive.

Cheryl: I wis referrin' to the Neptune Bar. So, fit wye did you bring me back here?

Doricula: To consummate our relationship.

Cheryl: Are you feel? I'm already engaged, ti Clint! He's geein me a ring the mor'n.

Doricula: How will he ken to phone here?

Cheryl: Nae that kind a' ring.

Doricula: I dinna ken fit you see in him. He's nae affa bright.

Cheryl: Aye he is. He passed his eleven plus. Last wik.

Doricula: Forget Clint. You're mine's now

Cheryl: No way! I dinna ging oot wi' al'er men.

Doricula: Why nae?

Cheryl: I hid a bad experience.

Doricula: Fan?

Cheryl: Widdensday.

Doricula: They say al'er men mak the best lovers.

Cheryl: No they dinna.

Doricula: It depends on the setting.

Cheryl: It wis a doorway.

Doricula: That can be romantic.

Cheryl: Nae in St Clement Street. Wi' a boy peein' on your fit.

Doricula: Fa wis it? I mean the boy makkin' love ti yi. Nae the een peein' on your fit.

Cheryl: It wis the same boy. I dinna ken fa he wis. It wis pitch black. He wis' a' wrinkled. Like a shammy. And he couldna', you ken …

Doricula: Get it up?

Cheryl: Find his wallet.

Doricula: Did he nae say his name?

Cheryl: No. But he did hae a name badge.

Doricula: Fit did it say?

Cheryl: "Woolmanhillati".

Kingseat: Hazelheid! Wis that you?

(Hazelheid coughs and staggers into view)

Hazelheid: Hud on! I can explain! It wis the blackoot. I didna hae my glaises. They wis a' slivers. I didna ken it wis Cheryl.

Cheryl: Uncle?

Kingseat: He's nae your uncle.

Cheryl: He's the spittin' image.

Hazelheid: No, it's true. I'm nae your uncle.

Cheryl: I ken you're nae actually my uncle.

Hazelheid: I'm your da.

Cheryl: No, you're nae. My da wis ca'd Barnes.

Hazelheid: Barnes Noble?

Cheryl: Aye.

Hazelheid: Wis?

Cheryl: Aye. He's deid. He got squashed wi' a tunk at Dunkirk.

Kingseat: He tried ti bla' up a Jerry tunk? Fit bravery!

Cheryl: No, it wis oors. He wis hidin' underneath.

Kingseat: How come he didna get oot aneeth it?

Cheryl: He didna ken it hid started. He wis deef.

Kingseat: Fae a' the explosions?

Cheryl: Fae a' the wax.

Hazelheid: Onywye, that wisna your da'. I'm your da.

Kingseat: Me ana'.

Cheryl: You're baith my da?

Kingseat: Aye. No, one o' us is. We baith hid sex wi' baith Bunties. Nae a' at once.

Cheryl: Oh my God! So it could be either een o' you?

Kingseat: Aye. Or somebody else.

Cheryl: Three da's?

Hazelheid: No, jist one.

Doricula: Come on, Cheryl, We need ti get oot of the light and inti the coffin.

Cheryl: I'm nae ga'n in that coffin! I'm nae a Vampire ...

Doricula: You nearly are. I drunk your bleed.

Cheryl: I'm still nae getting' in there. It smells like a turd.

Doricula: There's nae turds in it. Well, there might be one. A'right - jist pit on this sunblock instead. (Hands her sunblock).

Cheryl: Dis sunblock work?

Doricula: Of course it works. I use it a' the time.

Hazelheid: Fit? You ging oot in the sun?

Doricula: How else wid I get my messages? OK, that's enough. I'm awa ti' my kip. (He gets in the coffin)

[Sound effect: Coffin lid closing. Followed by chapping].

Doricula: (Muffled) Fit?

Hazelheid: Open up! Me and Kingseat hiv a little something for you.

[Sound effect: Coffin lid opening].

Doricula: Fit? The old 'stake through the heart'? You ken that disna work.

Kingseat: He said it dis.

Doricula: Let me tell you something aboot Mr. "Hazelheid".

Hazelheid: Dinna listen ti him! Mind fit I said – he's playin' us against each ither.

Doricula: He farts in the bath and collects the bubbles in a bottle.

Kingseat: No he disna. I div, and it's a cup.

Hazelheid: Actually it's true. I lied afore.

Kingseat: A bottle? How can you be that accurate?

Hazelheid: Practice.

Cheryl: That's disgusting.

Hazelheid: Wait till you open the bottle.

Doricula: He's also a German spy.

Hazelheid: No, I'm nae.

Doricula: Aye you are. You wis sent here by Hitler to set up a secret society.

Kingseat: The Woolmanhillati?

Cheryl: That's fit his name badge said.

Doricula: Exactly. Fit wye div you think he wants to kill me?

Kingseat: Because you're a vampire.

Doricula: No. He's got heaps a' vampire chums. The Nazzies hiv a hale Vampire Battalion. He wants ti steal my inheritance. And gie it ti Hitler.

Kingseat: Fit inheritance?

Doricula: The een that Robert the Bruce gid me. The Common Good Fund.

Hazelheid: Rubbish. It's nae for Hitler! It's to build a better Aiberdeen!

Doricula: It's ti build a better Führermuseum.

Hazelheid: It's a' lies! I telt you he wid dee that! Come on, Kingseat! Dinna be stupid. Fit div you think is more likely? My vision of an all-concrete Aiberdeen, or the ravings of a half-deid bat?

Kingseat: Eh … I'm ga'n wi' the bat.

Hazelheid: OK. You leave me nae choice. (Pulls out a Luger pistol)

Kingseat: Hazelheid! Pit doon that gun! Oh, is that a Luger? Gie's a shottie.

[Sound effect: Loud gunshot]

(Silence for a few seconds)

Cheryl: Ow. My lugs is dirlin' again. Kingseat! Are you deid?

Kingseat: No. He missed!

Cheryl: Fa got shot?

Kingseat: That's Hazelheid!

Cheryl: Mair like Hazel Nae Heid.

Kingseat: Did you shoot him?

Doricula: No. My gun's upstairs.

Cheryl: He must have shot himsel'.

(Enter Wallfield, from hiding)

Wallfield: No, actually that wis me. Sorry!

Doricula: Wallfield! Far did you come fae?

Cheryl: You shot my da'.

Wallfield: Jist one o' them. He wis ga'n ti shoot your ither da.

Cheryl: Oh, Wallfield! You're right brave. I think I misjudged you! (Grabs his arm)

Wallfield: Hey, cut it oot.

Cheryl: I aye thought you funcied me.

Wallfield: I div. But Clint's my best friend. He'd kill me.

Kingseat: Excuse me: on that note - div you want to hear the bad news, the bad news, or the bad news?

Cheryl: Eh ... the ... bad news.

Kingseat: OK. Clint telt me and your ither dad he wis brakkin' aff the engagement.

Cheryl: Fit wye?

Kingseat: Because one of us might have accidentally mentioned that maybe he's your brother.

Cheryl: Fit? How could he maybe be my brither?

Kingseat: Because him and me had sex with baith Bunties.

Cheryl: Clint had sex wi' my ma?

Kingseat: No (points to Hazelheid) him and me.

Cheryl: Clint hid sex wi you two?

Kingseat: No, me and Hazelheid hid sex wi baith Bunties.

Cheryl: Fit, a' the gither?

Kingseat: No, no. Nae mair than three at a time.

Cheryl: How wid that mak Clint my brither?

Kingseat: Because the Bunties is twins.

Cheryl: I nivver kint that.

Kingseat: I dinna think they kint. They wis adopted.

Cheryl: Is that why they're baith ca'd Bunty?

Kingseat: No – their biological mum wisna good wi' names.

Cheryl: Fit wis her name?

Kingseat: Bunty.

Cheryl: Fit's the other bad news?

Kingseat: Clint said he wis brakkin aff the engagement.

Cheryl: Again? Fit wye this time?

Kingseat: Same as last time. Because you funcy Doricula.

Cheryl: Gads! He's al' enough to be my great... great... great great ...

Doricula: OK, enough greats. You made your point.

Cheryl: ... great great great granda'. Fit's the ither bad news?

Kingseat: Me and Hazelheid asked him to help us save you, and he refused.

Cheryl: Why?

Kingseat: Same reason.

Cheryl: Far is he?

Kingseat: He went ti the Ice Rink.

Cheryl: Ice Rink? Ice Rink? I'll gie him Ice Rink! I'll kill him!

Kingseat: Oh, aye, that's number four. He's deid.

Cheryl: I'll gie him deid! I'll kill him! How come he's deid?

Kingseat: The Ice Rink got burned doon.

Wallfield: Wid an Ice Rink nae jist pit itsel' oot?

Kingseat: Nae fan a Heinkel crashes inti it.

Wallfield: Wis it a wifey pilot?

Kingseat: No, it got shot doon wi' a Spitfire. We seen it happenin'.

Cheryl: Oh. Poor Clint. That wis right unlucky.

Kingseat: I ken. They wis supposed ti be bombing Dundee.

Wallfield: But that means there's good news.

Cheryl: Fit good news?

Wallfield: Well, you ken how Clint's your brother? And he dumped you? And got bla'n up and drooned?

Cheryl: Drooned?

Wallfield: Aye, fan the ice melted. Well, I assume.

Cheryl: OK, I get it. How the hell is that good news?

Wallfield: Well, now, wi' him bein' burnt ti a crisp, and deid ... you and me can be the gither. Div you funcy gettin' mairied?

Cheryl: (sarcastic) Oh, that's affa romantic.

Wallfield: I ken. Thanks.

Cheryl: No. That's aboot as romantic as a fart in the lug.

Wallfield: A fit?

Cheryl: No, a fart. Clint used ti dee that. It tickles.

Wallfield: Gads. OK. How aboot this? (Gets down on one knee). Div you want ti get mairied or no?

Cheryl: A'right, OK then. I suppose so (They cuddle).

Doricula: A'right you two. Get a coffin. Can I get my gun back?

Wallfield: Nae fears! Keep back (he points it).

Doricula: There's nae point pointin' that at me. Bullets dinna touch me.

[Sound effect: Loud gunshot]

Doricula: (holding his upper arm) Ow!! My airm! That wis sair. Wis that a silver bullet?

Wallfield: No, it wis leed.

Doricula: That widna work. Unless … wis it holy?

Wallfield: Aye. It wis aff the roof a' Beechgrove.

Doricula: Well, if you dinna mind, I'm ga'n ti Woolmanhill.

Wallfield: You'll need a note fae your GP.

Kingseat: I can gie you a note (looks for his pen). Fit's your name?

Doricula: I'm nae ga'n ti A & E. I'm ga'n ti the blood bank.

(Exit Doricula)

Cheryl: So, fit happens now?

Kingseat: Well, first he'll find oot blood banks hinna been invented. Then he'll die. Then he'll start to decompose.

Cheryl: No, I mean aboot the Common Good Fund.

(Enter Doricula)

Doricula: I heard that.

Cheryl: Oh, ye'r back. That wis quick.

Doricula: I didna go yet. I'll tell you fit. I'll split the Common Good Fund wi' the toon. I'll tak seven billion quid and Aiberdeen can keep the ither seven billion.

Wallfield: Can I hae the twelve and six?

Doricula: Fit for?

Wallfield: An engagement ring.

Kingseat: Hud on (searches in Hazelheid's jacket pockets). Here!

Wallfield: You canna rob a corpse like that!

Kingseat: No, this is Clint's mother's ring. So, Cheryl, it's yours now (hands it to Cheryl)

Cheryl: Hey, Wallfield – I'll sell you it.

Wallfield: How much?

Cheryl: Twelve and six.

Wallfield: (to Doricula) See?

Doricula: OK, I'll gie you twelve and six. On one condition.

Wallfield: Fit?

Doricula: If a'body donates bleed. I'm doon ti my last crepuscle.

Kingseat: Blood cell?

Doricula: Sunset.

Kingseat: Hud on. Afore onybody starts donating bleed - fit aboot Midstocket?

Doricula: I dinna want Midstocket. I'm starting to feel fint. I need bleed... The toon can keep the land.

Kingseat: Perfect! OK, I'm ga'n to be the new Provost. We'll use the income ti mak Hazelheid's dream come true. Ti honour the City's architectural heritage. We'll start wi' building prefabs! And then we'll burn the trams! Fa needs trams? And then, we'll turn the jin't station inti shops. And we'll turn Union Terrace Gardens into a skateboard rink. In less than a century we'll be the UK's City a' Culcher! Dundee winna hae a ghosters!

[Sound effect: Gravelly sound]

Cheryl: Fit's that?

Doricula: (Weakly) That wis probably Archibald Simpson turning in his grave. Spickin' a fit, can somebody phone me a taxi – afore I turn inti a deid bat?

Kingseat: There's nae taxis oot here.

Doricula: How did you get oot?

Kingseat: A tandem.

Doricula: That'll hae to dee. Will you ging wi' me?

Kingseat: A'right – but I'm takkin' the back seat!

Chapter 12 - This evening

Wallfield and Cheryl's house: Burnieboozle Crescent.

Wallfield, Cheryl and Clint in the living room.

Clint: This is nice, reminiscing aboot the past.

Wallfield: Fit else wid we reminisce aboot? The future?

Cheryl: Fit's the maiter wi' you?

Wallfield: How come I hid to pye for the taxi? I'm a pensioner.

Clint: I offered ti pye. He didna tak cards.

Wallfield: He did tak cards. Jist nae Morrison's gift cards.

Cheryl: Come on, Wallfield, it's a special occasion. It's been seventy-four year.

Wallfield: Fitever.

Clint: It wis you that invited me.

Wallfield: Aye, but I didna ken I'd be oot eight quid and ten pee.

Clint: I thought he said eight quid.

Wallfield: Aye, wi the tip.

Cheryl: Wallfield – get into the spirit.

Wallfield: A' right, I will. Keep your hair on. (Picks up the remote)

Cheryl: Fit are you deein'?

Wallfield: Pittin' on Fear Factor.

Cheryl: Stop it! Clint – fit wid you like ti drink?

Clint: Fit hiv you got?

Cheryl: (looking in the drinks cabinet) Oh, there's a'thin'. Ribena.

Clint: Onything alcoholic?

Cheryl: Aye. Schlöer.

Clint: That's nae alcoholic.

Cheryl: Aye it is. If you leave it open. In the airing cupboard. Since the World Cup final.

Clint: Fit, 2014?

Cheryl: 1966.

Clint: Hiv you onything that's nae sweet?

Cheryl: There's a BabyCham left o'er.

Clint: Fae fit?

Cheryl: My christening.

Clint: Hiv you got beer?

Cheryl: There's a Sweetheart Stout.

Clint: That'll dee (takes it). Thanks. Oh no! You're kidding.

Cheryl: Fit?

Clint: That's my mum on the can.

Wallfield: Wis your mum a model?

Clint: Aye, in 1888.

Cheryl: I think stout keeps. Here.

Clint: Ta. Div you hae a tin opener?

Cheryl: Fit for? Is there nae a ring-pull?

Clint: Nivver mind. Let's jist spick. Is it nae funny?

Cheryl: Fit? That I dinna hae a tin opener?

Clint: No, that we're a' still alive - at a hundred and twenty eight.

Wallfield: Well, me and Cheryl got bitten by Doricula.

Clint: Did you turn into vampires?

Wallfield: No, we didna. Fit aboot you?

Clint: I never got bitten.

Wallfield: Maybe you caught something aff that stripper.

Clint: I never touched her.

Wallfield: Or her punts.

Clint: I never touched them either.

Wallfield: So, fit's your excuse?

Clint: It must be something in my diet.

Cheryl: Like fit?

Clint: Rowies. Spickin' a fit, I'll hae mine toasted.

Cheryl: We hinna got a toaster.

Clint: Jist warm it up in the oven.

Cheryl: We hinna got an oven.

Clint: A'right, jist a cal' rowie. Wi' a suppie jam. Dinna tell me you dinna hae jam.

Cheryl: There's heaps a' jam. Damson...

Clint: Gads. Fit else?

Cheryl: Jist damson. Heaps.

Clint: A'right.

[Sound effect: Clink of plates]
Cheryl: There you go

Clint: That's jist jam. Far's the rowie?

Cheryl: We dinna hae ony rowies

Clint: Fit? He invited me back for a rowie.

Wallfield: Aye, you wis bringing the rowies.

Clint: You could have said that in Morrison's.

Wallfield: Fit for? Morrison's wis oot a rowies.

Clint: A'right, never mind the rowie.

Cheryl: Fit aboot a Rich Tea?

Clint: No, that's a' right.

Cheryl: A Hob Nob?

Clint: No, never mind. Come here, sit doon. So, you're still biding in the same hoose.

Wallfield: Aye. This wis my ma and da's hoose.

Clint: Fit happened ti them?

Wallfield: They're up the stairs.

Clint: Oh, they're alive?

Wallfield: I hope no. They're beeried in the bomb shelter.

Clint: Fit happened ti' the plot in the Trinity Cemetery?

Wallfield: It turned oot it wis at the Trinity Center.

Clint: Hiv you done much wi' the hoose?

Wallfield: Oh, aye heaps. We pinted the lobby.

Cheryl: Aye, in 1957. Wallfield's nae much o' a handyman.

Wallfield: I am sut! I pit up pelmets in 1968. And I teen doon the pulley.

Cheryl: Aye, but you left the mangle.

Wallfield: I thought you loved the mangle.

Cheryl: It disna work.

Wallfield: I thought mangles wis indestructible.

Cheryl: They are. But we jist hiv one sink. I never did get my dream.

Clint: Fit, a Poggenpohl kitchen?

Cheryl: No, an inside lavvie.

Wallfield: Fit's wrang wi' the een in the bomb shelter?

Cheryl: Nithing. Jist your ma and da in the bath.

Wallfield: But they're covered wi' mulch.

Cheryl: Except for his airse. A'right - enough aboot the hoose. So, tell us - fit happened to you? How come you didna get killed at the ice rink?

Clint: I went ti the een on George Street. So fit happened ti a'body?

Cheryl: Abody fa?

Clint: Van Hazelheid?

Wallfield: You ken he wis your da' – right?

Clint: That's fit he said. Is he still alive?

Wallfield: I doot it. It wis seventy-four year ago.

Clint: Oh aye, right enough.

Wallfield: Plus I blew his heid aff.

Clint: How?

Wallfield: Wi' a gun

Clint: No, I mean fit wye?

Wallfield: Oh. He wis ga'n ti shoot your ither da.

Clint: Kingseat? Fit came a' him?

Cheryl: He got bla'n up.

Clint: Oh, 'ta shame. Wi' a bomb?

Wallfield: No, a cooker.

Clint: Fit aboot Doricula?

Wallfield: I shot him ana'.

Clint: Far aboot?

Wallfield: Cruden Bay.

Clint: No, far aboot on his body?

Wallfield: His airm.

Clint: Dis that work wi' Vampires?

Wallfield: Nae normally. The bullet must have hit an artery. He lost that much blood, he needed a transfusion.

Clint: Fa wid gie a Vampire a transfusion?

Cheryl: Me.

Clint: You?

Cheryl: Aye. He already hid half my bleed, so I jist gid him a suppie mair.

Clint: Why did you nae jist let him bleed oot?

Wallfield: Because he promised me twelve and six.

Clint: Fit for?

Wallfield: Ti buy Cheryl's mum's ring fae Cheryl. Ti gie ti Cheryl.

Clint: So he gid you the twelve and six?

Wallfield: Aye. Actually Doricula turned oot ti be a' right. He split the Common Good fund wi' Kingseat.

Clint: Fit did Kingseat want wi' the Common Good Fund?

Wallfield: Ti turn the Granite City into the Cement City.

Clint: He's certainly done that.

Wallfield: Nae quite. Wait till you see fit they dee wi' Marischal Square. And the Art Gallery. And the Triple Kirks. And the Capitol. And the al' Bruce Millers.

Cheryl: Tell him the really weird thing.

Clint: Fit?

Wallfield: The transfusion cured him. And even mair weird, it cured a' the folk he'd bitten.

Clint: Cured them a' fit?

Cheryl: Drinking bleed.

Wallfield: But it didna cure him fae drinking a' the gither. He jist switched ti whisky.

Clint: Fit wis his favourite?

Wallfield: Doubles.

Cheryl: He ended up wi' an affa reed nose. Like Rudolph.

Clint: Did he ging back ti Cluj?

Cheryl: No – he wisna fae Cluj. Nae originally. He wis Scottish. He bade on in Aiberdeen.

Clint: Deein' fit?

Cheryl: It wis something ti dee wi' fitba.

Wallfield: He wis the former Don's Manager.

Clint: How div you stop bein' the 'former' manager?

Wallfield: Shut up. Onywye, that wis back fan the Dons could play fitba. And then he went awa doon sooth.

Clint: Far? Cove?

Wallfield: No, Manchester. He jist retired nae lang ago.

Clint: And far is he now?

Wallfield: He's back here.

Clint: Far aboot?

(Cheryl and Wallfield look at each other, then up)

Both: He's up in the bath!

[Music: Doricula Theme]

Afterlogue – Present evening.

Aiberdeen beach, in front of the Inversnecky
[Sound effect: Surf]

Cheryl and Wallfield are walking arm in arm on the sand. They stop at a groyne.

Cheryl: Ken ess, Wallfield. I nivver kint you wis si' romantic. I jist love strolling along the beach. Fit's the maiter?

Wallfield: (He has spotted something) Is that a bottle?

Cheryl: Aye, it is a bottle. Bloody minkers.

Wallfield: No, I dinna think onybody drapped it.

Cheryl: How nae?

Wallfield: It says 'Dazzle'.

Cheryl: Oh, fit rare! That could be worth a fortune.

(They both bend over and examine it closely).

Cheryl: Fit yi deein'? Dinna open it! (Wallfield opens it). Gads! Fit's a' that white stuff?

(Wallfield samples it with his finger, tastes it).

Wallfield: Brie.

Cheryl: Tattie?

Wallfield: No, cheese. Wait a minute. I think this proves your da' wisna squashed wi a tunk. It wis a suicide.

Cheryl: How div you ken?

Wallfield: There's a note.

(The End).

Historical and Local Notes

As stated on the first page, 'Doricula' is a work of fiction. Places and incidents, where real, are used fictitiously. Any resemblance between the characters and any individual – living or dead – is coincidental. Northeast readers, however, will recognize some character names. In the interest of transparency, the following (again in order of appearance) is a list of real versus invented characters. As far as I know, none of real characters behaved as portrayed.

Barnes Noble – fictional. The "letter hame" has appeared in many iterations, from Sandy Scott's 1912 missive from the South Pole to his mum (Temporary Fualt, 1978), through First Officer Pox's Star Trek Star Log (Temporary Fualt – the Movie, 1980), to ad hoc versions at AU Medical School dinners and reunions over the years.

Reverend Deverend Vale - fictional. First appeared in 'Dr Fa and the Dorics', but in various guises has featured in many Northeast skits since the late seventies.

Cheryl Noble and Clint Eastneuk – fictional. Both first appeared in a sketch entitled 'Lemmings' in the early 1980s, and in 'Dr Fa and the Dorics'.

Wallfield – fictional.

Donnie J Macleodmouth – fictional. Any resemblance to Donald J Trump (whose mother, Mary Anne MacLeod, was born in Lewis) is imaginary.

Coont Doricula - fictional. Any resemblance, in his later life, to a famous son of Govan is purely accidental.

Arthur Bean – a salute to the late Arthur Bean, my parents' contemporary, and Westray Road neighbour. Arthur drove Aberdeen Corporation buses, and was one of the funniest men I've known.

Operator – fictional. Based on characters from Methlick Cabs in 'Dr Fa and the Dorics'.

Abraham Van Hazelheid – fictional. Hazelhead (pronounced 'Hazelheid') park was originally part of the freedom lands granted to the city in 1319. The land became privately owned (not by the Lord Provost) and was indeed bought back by the council in 1920.

Brother Duthie – fictional. The Duthie Park was donated to the City of Aberdeen by Elizabeth Crombie Duthie (of the shipbuilding family) in 1880. http://www.duthieonline.com/user/image/otherfamousduthies.pdf

Athol Benzie existed. Isaac Benzie Senior established Isaac Benzie, originally a drapery, in George Street, Aberdeen in 1894 – see http://www.housefraserarchive.ac.uk/company/?id=c1374. His sons, Isaac and Athol continued to run it after his death in 1922. Isaac Junior died in 1935. A short film featuring the original Isaac Benzie store can be seen at the National Library of Scotland Screen Archive http://ssa.nls.uk/film/2152. See also 'The Doric Column' for an excellent review of the history of St Nicholas and George streets, and a commentary on the 'City Fathers' Folly' – the characteristically idiotic and short-sighted decision to destroy the thoroughfare and many of its historic buildings in favor of a low-grade indoor shopping mall, the St. Nicholas Centre http://mcjazz.f2s.com/GeorgeSt.htm.

Peter Craigmyle, the "fearless Aberdonian" (from Oldmeldrum), was indeed a well-known referee who officiated in league, cup and international matches from 1918 to the 1940s.

The Giulianotti and Brattisani families settled in Scotland from Parma in Italy in the 1880s. Giulio Giulianotti and his wife Rosa Brattisani were well-known for their excellent ice cream, as well as their fish & chip shops.

Brother Esslemont – Peter Esslemont and William Macintosh opened E & M's in 1873. Originally in Broad Street, it moved about eight feet to Union Street in the 1920s. Most of the author's Aberdeen Grammar School uniforms were purchased there.

Brothers James and William Hall founded Hall, Russell & Co., with Thomas Russell and James Cardno Couper, in 1864. During the 2nd World War Hall Russell built smaller vessels (corvettes and frigates) for the Royal Navy. The Hall Russell shipyard was bombed on July 12, 1940 (see below).

Brother Wood – Sir Ian Wood's grandfather, William, co-founded the ship repair and marine engineering firm, Wood & Davidson in the early 1900s. Whether he was in Aberdeen in 1940 isn't certain.

Dr. John Kingseat – fictional. The Kingseat Lunatics Asylum opened in 1904, and finally closed in 1994. During the second world war it was occupied by the British Royal Navy.

The Aiberdeen Illuminati (Woolmanhillati) – of course it exists. As Hazelheid observed, "… responsibility can't be entrusted to a bunch of elected halfwits with personal agendas."

The Common Good Fund – From Wikipedia, the free encyclopedia.
(http://en.wikipedia.org/wiki/Common_Good_Fund, accessed Jan 3rd 2015)
"Aberdeen's Common Good Fund is a fund to benefit the people of Aberdeen,
Scotland. It was created as a result of Robert the Bruce granting the cities Great
Charter in 1319, after they sheltered him during his days of outlaw. In 2005, the
value of the fund was £31 million."
[MJJ – so what happened to the other 13,969,000,000?]
"Along with the Great Charter, Bruce gave Aberdeen the Forest of Stocket (now
the Mid Stocket area of the city), in return for a yearly rent. As a result of the
finances generated from the forest, the Common Good Fund was created to
benefit the people of the city."
"The fund helped to create Marischal College by giving land to George Keith, 5th
Earl Marischal to help him build the institution; it helped the people during the
1640 plague and also gave funds to Aberdeen Art Gallery, the Central Library,
Aberdeen Royal Infirmary and the purchase of Hazlehead Park."
"There are 195 other Common Good Funds around Scotland although the
number and size of each has dwindled over the years due to mismanagement,
lack of interest, *and illegal sales to private interests* [MJJ – my italics]. See "Who
Owns Scotland" and "Common Good—A Quick Guide" by Andy Wightman."
(http://www.andywightman.com/docs/commongoodguide_v6.pdf)

The Air Raid on Aberdeen, July 12 1940
For a detailed description of recorded air raids on Aberdeen and bomb hits,
throughout WWII, see
https://maps.google.co.uk/maps/ms?ie=UTF8&vps=1&authuser=0&oe=UTF8&ms
a=0&msid=204031601317387489834.00048e01602ad2ff1d387
July 12, 1940. "3 High Explosive bombs are dropped on Urquhart Road, as well as
two on properties in Roslin Terrace. Unexploded bombs are found on the railway
line close to the King Street Bridge."
Bear in mind that – during wartime - not all bomb hits were recorded: particularly
those from unexploded bombs. An unexploded bomb also landed in the back
garden of the Hendersons' house at 27 Jasmine Terrace on July 12. By
coincidence, the Hendersons' son was one of the engineers who defused and
removed it.
My dad, James Jamieson, was 11 years old and en route home for lunch from
Frederick Street School to Jasmine Terrace when he heard the unmistakable
interrupted drone of a Heinkel He-111's engines overhead. He barely made it
home before the stick described above landed. He remembers vividly the sound
of the explosions, the house appearing to lift from its foundations, dust and
plaster flying, his mother screaming – and then the silence.

A description of the raid, and the downing of a Heinkel He-111 onto the brand
new ice rink is at http://forum.12oclockhigh.net/showthread.php?t=

"12th July, 1940. Enemy aircraft appeared suddenly with no warning at 12:45 PM and launched an attack on the Hall Russell shipyards. Approximately 16 High Explosive bombs are dropped on Hall Russell, with the majority hitting the Boiler Works. A High Explosive bomb also hits the London Boat at Waterloo Quay. 25 bodies are brought to the ARP Emergency Mortuary at Berryden Road."

"13810 9./KG26 Heinkel He 111H-3. Sortied to attack Leuchars airfield with harbour installations at Broughty Ferry, Dundee, as alternate. Shot down by Yellow Section No. 603 Squadron (Pilot Officer J. R. Caister, Pilot Officer G. K. Gilroy and Sergeant I. K. Arber) over Aberdeen 1.10 p.m. Crashed and burned out at the skating rink in South Anderson Drive. (Ff) Lt Herbert Huck, (Bf) Gefr Georg Kerkhoff, (Bm) Uffz Paul Plischke and (Beo) Fw August Skokan all killed. Aircraft 1H+FT a write-off. This crew was buried in Graves 155, 150, 149, and 152 in the Old Churchyard at Dyce on July 16, 1940. They were not reinterred in the Soldatenfriedhof at Cannock Chase after the war."

Twenty five innocent merchantmen and civilian builders, murdered anonymously by otherwise talented young airmen, in support of an evil and ultimately worthless cause. Five young German sons; themselves killed by equally talented young British men, who disagreed with the cause. Fortunately, three-quarters of a century later, a mature world has learned from the tragedy and pointlessness of war, and the idiocies of ideology and theocracy. Aye, right.

"I am tired and sick of war. Its glory is all moonshine. It is only those who have neither fired a shot nor heard the shrieks and groans of the wounded who cry aloud for blood, for vengeance, for desolation. War is hell." - William Tecumseh Sherman

"Lands, titles, men, power... nothing" - Robert the Bruce. Actually, Randall Wallace.

"Will you shut up? I ken fit I'm deein'. You're the een that's trying, trying, trying – so ti spik" – The Spider.

Glossary

'Aiberdeen'	Translation
a' (aa)	of, every, all
aff	off
affa	awful, awfully
afore	before
airse	arse
ana'	also, as well
backie	back garden (alt. passenger ride on a bicycle seat)
backwards	intellectually challenged
bade	stayed, lived, resided
bahoochie	backside
bairn	baby
baith	both
bap	soft baked roll. Softie with flour.
beeried	buried
bide	stay, live, reside
bidey-in	common law wife
bla	blow
bogie	nasal mucus
boy	man
brak	break
breed	bread
buckie	periwinkle
bussies	bus fare
ca' (alt. cry)	(v) call, name
ca', canna	can't
ca'd	called / named
cairier	carrier
cal'	cold
cappy	ice-cream cone
cairy oot	carry out (alcohol, food), 'To Go'
casual	football hooligan
chappie	man
chappin'	knocking
cheer	chair
chick	cheek (facial feature & rudeness)
chored	stolen
clies	clothes
cloot	cloth
clout	knock, blow
closie (close)	passageway between attached buildings (e.g. tenements)

'Aiberdeen'	Translation
cludgie	toilet
cooch	couch, sofa, settee
Co-opy	Northern Cooperative Society
croon	crown
cumpy	campy, effeminate
cuppie	cup (when unqualified, = tea)
dazzie	glass marble
Dazzle	a dark soft drink (mfr. William Hay & Sons)
dee	do
dinna	don't
dirling	ringing
dis	does
div	do
doather	daughter
Dod, Doddie	George
doo	pigeon
doon	down
doot	doubt
dra'ers	drawers, underwear
dubs	earth, mud
een	one
Embra	Edinburgh
erse	arse
ess	this
fa	who
fa'	all
fae	from
fan	when
fa'n	falling
far, far aboot	where
feart	scared
feel	intellectually challenged
first fitting	first footing (a Hogmanay tradition)
fit	what, which
fit	foot
fit like?	how are you?
fit?	excuse me?
fitba	football
fleer	floor
floor, flooer	flour, flower
Foggie Loan	Aberchirder

'Aiberdeen'	Translation
forkytail	earwig
freen	friend
ga'n	going
gid	gave, went
gie	give
ging	go
gis	goes, give me
glaises	spectacles
gob	spit
goon	gown
greener	nasal mucus
greenie	drying green
grippy	cheap, tight fisted
grut (past tense of greet)	cried, wept
g'wan ...	go away and ...
haar	fog
hae	have
hale	whole
hame	home
hate	heat
Haudagain	an Aberdeen roundabout
heid	head
high heidyin'	boss, CEO, President
hindey, hindie	a long way
hing	hang
hinna	haven't
hiv	have
hogmanay	New Year's Eve
homer	handyman work, done on the side
how	why
hud	hold
hunkie	handkerchief
ile	oil
iv now, of now	at the moment
jandies	jaundice
jine	join
ken	know
kent, kint	knew
lavvie	toilet
loon	boy
lug	ear
lum	chimney

'Aiberdeen'	Translation
mair	more
maist	most
messages	groceries
min', mind	remember, mind
mine's	mine (i.e. belonging to me)
minker	white trash. gypsy, tinker.
min't	remembered
modrin	modern
mony	many
moo	mouth
mor'n's mor'n	tomorrow morning
nae	not, no
naewye	nowhere
neen	none
nippit	tight
ony	any
onywye	anyway, anywhere
palin' (paling)	fence
palled aroon'	was friends with
partan	young crab
pash, pish	urine
Peep Peep's	an Aberdeen bar, in the harbour area
pintin'	painting
pit	put
Pittodrie	Aberdeen Football Club's stadium
plooin'	ploughing
plook	facial furuncle (US 'zit')
pluff	blow (e.g. pea from a peashooter)
pooch	pocket
potted heid (hough)	head cheese
pra'n pluffer	prawn (shrimp) sheller
pucklie	few
pun	pound
punts	pants, underwear
pye	pay
quine	girl
reed cheese	cheddar
RGU	Robert Gordon University
sair	sore
seen	saw, soon
shammy	chamois

'Aiberdeen'	Translation
sharn	shit (usually cows')
sick kids	Royal Aberdeen Children's Hospital
simmit (simmet)	vest
sinted	scented
skitin'	sliding
skitters	diarrhoea
sma'	small
sna	snow
snotter	nasal mucus
softie	soft baked roll. Bap without flour dusting.
somewye	somewhere
sook	suck
sparkie	electrician
spaver	trouser zip
spick, spik	speak
spile	spoil
spoonfae	spoonful
sput	spat
steen	stone
steep	soak
stirk	bullock or heifer
stovies	sauteed potatoes and (traditionally) leftover meat
suppie	small amount
sut	sat, so
tattiemasher	big dazzie (q.v.)
teen	took
telt	told
the gither	together
The Locarno	a former Aberdeen dance hall
The Malt Mill	an Aberdeen bar, on Holburn Street
The Moorings	an Aberdeen bar, in the harbour area
The Neptune Bar	an Aberdeen bar, near the harbour
The Palace	an Aberdeen dance hall
The Tivoli	an Aberdeen theatre
thochtie	small amount
thon	that
thruppence; thruppenny (n. or adj)	three pence (3d in pre-decimal money)
till	to
tool	towel
toon	town
toonser	from the town (of Aberdeen)
toor	tour; tower

'Aiberdeen'	Translation
toorie	wool hat
Trades' Fortnight	July holidays
trap	hook-up (e.g. a lady escorted home from the Palace)
unty	aunt
weet	wet
wick, wik	week
wid	wood
wifie	woman
winna	won't
wint	gone, want, went
wis	was
wisna	wasn't
wrang	wrong
wringing	wet
wye	way

Mike Jamieson September, 2016

Made in the USA
San Bernardino, CA
10 April 2016